Before the Storm

The Formative Years of
America's Last Great Band

Robert Boyd

Before the Storm

Cover Photo: Matt LaCross

Cover Design: M.A. Rehman

Author Photo: Sarah Boyd

For my loving and supportive wife;
"the editor."

Before the Storm

CONTENTS

"Nirvana, more than any other band, rocked way harder, had significant originality, while looking like guys you went to high school with. I think that was their secret. There was an inclusion that was long overdue, and it was what rock was supposed to be about."

Chris Cornell

"Every man has inside himself a parasitic being who is acting not at all to his advantage."

William S. Burroughs

"He was a wonderful person and he deserved a fulfilling life."

Krist Novoselic

PROLOGUE

"THE DEVIL'S WORKSHOP"

Upon entering Aberdeen, Washington, a remote town approximately 100 miles southwest of Seattle where the Wishkah and Chehalis Rivers converge, the blue-collar lifestyle becomes immediately evident. Founded by Samuel Benn in 1884 and incorporated on May 12, 1890, Aberdeen, also known as the "Gateway to the Olympic Peninsula," took its name from another fishing port; Aberdeen, Scotland. Although each municipality share the commonality of two rivers flowing into a larger body, the Washington town is surrounded by a dense and unforgiving wilderness while a sandy coastline borders Scotland's third most populous city.

The town's natural resources and accessibility to the Pacific Ocean led to exploitation and in 1894 the first sawmill was built. Aberdeen eventually experienced a timber boom in the early 20th century which resulted in an influx of population. Infamy followed due to the presence of numerous saloons, brothels, and gambling establishments. Ultimately, Aberdeen became synonymous with danger and was nicknamed "The Hellhole of the Pacific" and "The Port of Missing Men," the latter due to the many missing or murdered men who had been employed in the timber or maritime trades. Sailors who experienced the hazards of ports around the world had heard tales of Aberdeen and dreaded docking in the town for fear that they would never return to their ship. Any trepidations were justified and the term "Floater Fleet" was used to describe the corpses which were regularly pulled from the local rivers between 1902 and 1910. Overall, 124 bodies were found, however some historians estimate the deaths could have been as high as 200. William Gohl, a local union official, was later convicted of two murders, but was suspected of committing over a hundred more. Sentenced to a term of life, "The Ghoul of Grays Harbor" was later incarcerated at the Northern State Mental Hospital for the criminally insane in Sedro Woolley where he died in 1927.

Between the 1880s and 1910s, Aberdeen and other local towns, including Hoquiam and Cosmopolis, were carved out of the region's dense evergreen forests. Fed into the local rivers, timber then flowed into Grays Harbor which became the gateway for exportation to many countries throughout the world. A spur track, constructed by the Northern Pacific Railway in 1895, extended tracks from a main line into Aberdeen allowing for further convenience. The timber industry continued to flourish throughout the early 20th century and, at its height, Aberdeen was home to thirty-seven different timber mills and was recognized worldwide as a center for the exportation of lumber. By 1926 Grays Harbor exported 1.4 billion MBF (one MBF equals 1,000 board feet) of lumber, a record that stood for 100 years.

The timber industries' successes, like the rest of the advances in America at the turn of the century, were attributed to the sacrifices of the laborer. Those who sought the arduous employment in the northwest woods had little and were largely "womanless, voteless, and jobless," according to the Washington State Bureau of Labor in 1918. As trees were felled and America and other parts of the world were built during the Machine Age, injuries and deaths among loggers became as routine as the rain. Blood frequently soaked the earth. A dislodged branch falling to the ground, known as a "widow maker," was a common cause of devastation and grief. According to a report completed by the Safety Board of Washington State in 1920, the timber industry was described as "more deadly than war." Along with MBF, records were also tallied to track death. In 1923 alone, logging accidents accounted for 215 deaths in Washington State.

Like timber, brothels remained an accessibility for decades in Aberdeen. Nearly one hundred prostitutes were employed at any given time, establishing a substrata within the town, while satisfying the desires of countless loggers and sailors. In an attempt to address the town's increasing notoriety, *Look* magazine described Aberdeen in 1952 as "one of the hotspots in America's battle against sin." In the same year, Nellie Curtis, a notorious madam, relocated her exploits from Seattle to Aberdeen and invested $25,000 toward the purchase of the Cass Hotel. Following renovations, the hotel was renamed the Curtis Hotel and quickly became a center for prostitution among the city's dozen brothels. Over time, Curtis wielded as much power within Aberdeen as most elected officials. Combatting the port town's unfavorable reputation became a priority and, by the late 1950s, a police crackdown put an end to prostitution and Curtis fled to West Seattle.

Slowly, as the natural resources in the Pacific Northwest approached depletion, the industries transitioned to automation, relocated, or closed entirely, and by the 1980s nearly every timber mill in Aberdeen had ceased operations. Due to the economic impact created by the loss of industry, the town struggled to stabilize. A once bustling downtown became largely inactive and storefronts were slowly emptied and boarded-up. Flea markets and secondhand shops became commonplace. As population increased in other parts of Washington, numerous homes in Aberdeen were abandoned and population declined by five percent between 1940 and 1970. High rates of alcoholism, drug addiction, and unemployment followed and, amid a perpetually cloudy and rainy climate, by the end of the 20th century Grays Harbor County had one of the highest rates of suicide in the United States.

As the United States surged toward a new millennium, Aberdeen's isolation and stagnation became palpable; a modern day hinterland. Sadly, it's a story that has become common for many small American towns as internal prosperity gradually declines due to change and external greed. Aberdeen residents began to navigate their common struggles, blind to the world. Concurrently, a majority of the town's youth were afforded few outlets post high school with the exception of a humble job. An acceptance of the downturn became the norm. As described by journalist Everett True in 2006, "Aberdeen feels lethargic. The products in the antique shops sum the place up: overused, dirty, and neglected."

This environment would eventually cultivate the last great American rock band of the 20th century - Nirvana. Now nearly forty years removed, would Nirvana have been capable of birth in a thriving, gentrified town? According to the first known article ever written on Nirvana, titled "It May Be the Devil and It May Be the Lord....But It Sure As Hell Ain't Human" and appearing in the August 1988 edition of the Seattle rock magazine *Backlash*, "And keep your ears tuned to Aberdeen, because idle towns are the Devil's workshop."

1

THE SEED AND THE TREE

Kurt Donald Cobain, the son of Donald and Wendy (née Fradenburg) Cobain, was born on February 20, 1967, at the Grays Harbor Community Hospital, in Aberdeen, Washington. Cobain's parents met in high school and had a shotgun wedding on July 31, 1966, in Coeur d'Alene, Idaho, soon after discovering that Wendy was pregnant. In September 1969, after briefly renting a small home in Hoquiam, Washington, the couple bought a 1,000 square foot, three bedroom, two-story residence, located one town over at 1210 East First Street in Aberdeen. The family's home was situated in a section of Aberdeen unceremoniously referred to by locals as "felony flats." Despite the derogatory nickname, the neighborhood consisted primarily of simple constructions, occupied by middle class families, and would remain Cobain's home throughout his early development.

Changes became routine for the young family and on April 24, 1970, Kimberly Cobain was born. The child was Kurt Cobain's only full sibling and the pair immediately established a close bond and even shared the same striking blue eyes and light blonde hair. The family quickly settled into an average life in Aberdeen and during the subsequent years, while Cobain's mother transitioned from employment as a waitress to a homemaker, his father was employed as a lead mechanic at a local Chevron station where his initial annual income was $6,000. Although he could have earned more at any of the remaining local timber mills, those not yet shuttered by the region's economic despair, Don chose safety over security. Financial strains eventually impacted Cobain's parents' marriage and, at times, family members stepped in to provide monetary assistance. Locally, a stagnant population and a declining timber industry created strain for most. Nationally, the country's commitment to the Vietnam War and a soaring inflation during the 1970s added to the financial woes of countless families, including the Cobains.

Those closest to Cobain described him as a happy and sensitive child, but also excitable. Movement was constant and at times he blamed his mischievous behaviors on his imaginary friend, "Boddah." In order to address their son's restlessness, the Cobains modified his diet, specifically by limiting his sugar intake and removing Red Dye Number Two. Cobain was also brought to his physician who concluded that intervention was necessary and the amphetamine Ritalin was prescribed. Some later attributed Cobain's struggle with addiction as an adult to the medication, although this is merely an assumption. Regardless, the choice to prescribe Ritalin to any child in the early 1970s was a controversial one. Although attention deficit hyperactivity disorder was presumed, Cobain never received a formal diagnosis and Ritalin was discontinued after less than three months when the effects, which included an imbalanced sleep cycle, caused him to fall asleep in school. Ultimately, his family just accepted his energetic personality.

Not everything was impacted by Cobain's patterns of hyperactivity and at a young age he began to exhibit artistic talents. Members of his immediate family sought to nurture the child's growing skill and routinely provided him with art supplies and encouragement. Cobain's bedroom resembled an art studio and free time was regularly spent drawing. His newest pieces were found taped to his bedroom wall or, in an even greater place of prominence, the kitchen refrigerator. Television shows exposed Cobain to ideas that he incorporated into his art and he began to master Disney characters such as Mickey Mouse, Donald Duck, and Goofy. On one occasion, his paternal grandfather, Leland Cobain, was so impressed with the child's artwork that he assumed it had been traced. Undeterred, Cobain immediately drew a detailed cartoon figure to prove his talent as his grandfather looked on in amazement. In addition to drawing, Cobain engaged in other forms of art including modeling clay and at the age of eight, using a Super 8 camera, he made his own "claymation" short films; a form of stop-motion animation.

Cobain's happiness and extroverted nature were infectious and as his parents' first child, and also the first grandchild on either side of the family, he was surrounded by love and adoration throughout his formative years. Random Super 8 movies filmed by his family depicted Cobain as a healthy and handsome child rarely seen without a smile. He later described his early childhood as one of happiness met by few obstacles. With evident supports and a vast imagination, Cobain envisioned a future with infinite opportunities. "Up until I was about eight-years-old I had an extremely happy childhood - a really good one," Cobain explained in 1992. "I had everything in focus, I knew exactly what I was going to do and nothing could stop me and I knew that I could do whatever I want."

In February 1976, just one week before Cobain's ninth birthday, his mother informed Don Cobain that she planned to seek a divorce. Wendy immediately fled from the family's house leaving Don alone to explain the situation to their confused children. Increasing strain between the pair led to her decision, specifically financial stress and Wendy's annoyance with Don's constant involvement in local sports, however her actions surprised many within the family. Don assumed Wendy's frustration with the marriage would subside and, although he moved out on March 1, Don only rented a room by the week in Hoquiam. "I started to mature," Wendy later described. "Is that all there is? Is this my life? I haven't done anything with my life." To his dismay, Don was officially served with divorce papers less than one month later. Even after the ink from their signatures had dried and the dissolution of their marriage was finalized on July 9, Don still hoped to reconcile with Wendy. Ultimately, it would never happen.

Following the divorce, Don moved into his parents' home in the nearby town of Montesano. He kept a 1965 Ford truck and was ordered to pay $150 per month in child support, while Wendy kept a 1968 Camaro and the house the family once shared on East First Street of which her son had scrawled across his bedroom wall in graffiti, "I hate mom, I hate dad. Dad hates mom, mom hates dad. It simply makes you want to feel so sad. Mom sucks. Dad sucks." The divorce was far from amicable for the former couple and several instances of volatility between the pair during the initial months created further strain which ensured that their children would suffer most over time.

As an adult, Cobain acknowledged that his parents' divorce had a significant effect on his life. "I was ashamed of my parents," he acknowledged to journalist Jon Savage in 1993. "I couldn't face some of my friends at school anymore, because I desperately wanted to have the classic, you know, typical family. Mother, father. I wanted that security, so I resented my parents for quite a few years because of that."

Although Wendy was initially given legal custody of the children, within three months Cobain's disregard for his mother and her new boyfriend caused immediate strain. Seeking options for the child in the face of uncertainty, Cobain's parents determined by the year's end that their son would move in with his father and paternal grandparents, Leland and Iris Cobain, in their double-wide modular home. Weekends would be spent visiting his mother and sister, who remained in Aberdeen.

Happy to again be residing with his son, Don did whatever he could to provide normalcy. Guilty of the situation thrust upon his son, Don took the child to work with him and gave him gifts, including a Yamaha mini-bike. Any external happiness was brief and only masked Cobain's increasing despondency. Soon after, the pair moved into their own home and, in a further act to calm the emotionally unsettled child, Don insisted he and his son would always be together; just father and son. Despite his assurance, within eighteen months Don began to date and in 1978 he married Jenny Westby, a divorcee with two children. Although his stepmother had a caring demeanor toward the impressionable boy, Cobain remained faithful to his family and was hopeful that his parents would reunite.

Soon after his parents' divorce, those close to Cobain observed a personality change, including patterns of defiance. Unable to acclimate to his changing family, as time passed Cobain exhibited behavioral issues and at fourteen he informed a friend, "I'm going to be a superstar musician, kill myself, and go out in a flame of glory." Supervision had gradually decreased at his father's home and Cobain spent hours outside roaming the neighborhood. His internal struggles were manifested outwardly and he became rude to adults and his demeanor toward his peers had soured, including instances of bullying. Cobain eventually began meeting with a therapist who encouraged Wendy and Don to establish consistency for the preteen, including stable housing.

In June 1979, Cobain's father was granted legal custody of the twelve-year-old, however Cobain's unruliness and dismissive nature continued as he matured which created further strain within the home. Cobain was pushed into sports by his father, something Don held dear, despite the teenager's protests and desire to simply listen to music and watch endless hours of television. Over time Cobain joined the Little League, the track team, and the wresting squad. Although he exhibited slight athletic skill, particularly on the mat, Cobain's interests were elsewhere. He began to skip practices and had no desire to compete. On one occasion, in an act of defiance toward his father, Cobain allowed his opponent to pin him during an important wrestling match.

Exasperated by the scene before him, Don rose from his seat and stormed out of the gym.

By his fourteenth birthday, Cobain had moved into the home's renovated basement. Remnants of his artwork and stacks of albums stood out amongst the typically unkempt room. Cobain disregarded his assigned chores and isolated himself from the family. In an act of compounded frustration, Don grounded his son for a full year when the teen forgot to feed the family's dog. Consequently, each night as Cobain's father, stepmother, and step-siblings gathered around the television, the teen was directed to his bedroom. Cobain felt Don favored his new family and he believed his life in the basement was indicative of his detached place within the family. Eventually, in 1982, Cobain moved out of his father's home and developed a profound resentment toward his father and his new life which quickly limited their communication and had a lasting impact on their relationship. In later years, Don's only knowledge of his son came secondhand and from what he read in periodicals.

In hindsight, it's difficult to rationalize Cobain's extreme displeasure toward his father when, at a time during his formative years when his emotional needs were at their height, it was Don who took the child in. In his 2023 update to *Come As You Are: The Story of Nirvana*, Michael Azerrad noted that while Cobain would later have a "massive megaphone" to tell his tale, Don remained "a working guy in rural Washington State" and unable to provide any retort. "I think the sad part of the whole thing is that Kurt just really wanted to be with his mom," Cobain's stepmother noted in the 2015 documentary *Montage of Heck*. "And I don't know how anybody deals with having your whole family reject you."

By 1980, growth had proven to be insignificant for Cobain and therapy ceased. As with most teenagers, peers provided the greatest source of influence and Cobain was no different. Following the eighth grade, he began to experiment with marijuana which became part of his daily life and quickly led to carelessness. Marijuana had a profound impact and he exclaimed at the time that it was "something I will do the rest of my life!" By the eleventh grade, with the exception of art class, Cobain had little interest in his cumulative academic performance and he began cutting class regularly or skipping school entirely. Friendships were also largely inconsistent. "I felt more and more alienated - I couldn't find friends I was compatible with at all," Cobain described in 1992. "Everyone was eventually going to become a logger, and I knew I wanted to do something different. I wanted to be some kind of artist." Art class became the only reason Cobain attended school, while days outside of school were largely spent pursuing and subsequently smoking marijuana and drinking alcohol. He later expressed an affinity for the movie *Over the Edge* about a group of defiant teens living in an isolated town who rebel against parents and local authorities in a chaotic finale. Cobain's own patterns of anti-social behavior led to his first arrest in July 1985 when he was charged with "malicious mischief" for spray painting the side of a building in Aberdeen with the phrase "Ain't got no how watchamacallit." Basis for the statement is unclear. Hours after being photographed and fingerprinted, Cobain was released from custody once he provided an Officer with a written confession in which he acknowledged, "Now I see how silly it was for me to have done this." He avoided jail and was sentenced to a thirty day suspended sentence and ordered to pay a $180 fine. Cobain's failure to pay the fine would contribute to his brief detainment by law enforcement officials once again approximately ten months later.

As Cobain's exploits continued, education had become a weight in his life. Adding to his struggles, address changes led to transfers between schools in Grays Harbor County. The last school Cobain would attend was the J.M. Weatherwax High School, commonly referred to as Aberdeen High School. Overtime his school attendance had fluctuated and when he was present his academic effort was poor. With little time or options remaining as Cobain's high school career came to a close, school officials warned him that if he did not begin to apply himself he would not graduate. An art scholarship even became a possibility despite his poor performance in general classes. Ultimately, in May 1985, just weeks prior to what would have been his originally scheduled graduation, Cobain withdrew from high school after discovering he owed nearly two years worth of academic credits in order to acquire a high school diploma. Although Cobain then enrolled at an alternative high school, with the hope that the added support would be beneficial, he withdrew two weeks later.

Friction became routine wherever Cobain laid his head and during the subsequent years, after leaving his father's home in 1982, he lived with several family members and friends. Cobain also returned to his mother's home, however his academic decline created additional friction between the pair resulting in further housing instability.

Like her son, Wendy had also changed and was no longer the grounded maternal presence she once was. A pattern of alcohol use began and she frequented local taverns. On occasion, and contrary to her past maternal ideals, she provided Cobain and his friends with alcohol. As an attractive woman approaching middle age, Wendy relished the reactions she received from young men; something that embarrassed her introverted son. Her socialization outside the home was typical for a single woman and several men entered her life, including a volatile longshoreman who broke her arm during an alcohol fueled argument.

In February 1984, Wendy established a relationship with a longshoreman named Pat O'Connor. Although the pair were married within six months, their union was far from harmonious and arguments were routine. On one occasion, Wendy believed that O'Connor had been unfaithful when he returned home smelling of another woman. Seething with anger, she attempted unsuccessfully to load a firearm, all the while in the presence of her son and daughter, allowing O'Connor time to flee from the home. Soon after she calmed, Wendy collected every firearm from within the home. Cobain and his sister then watched as their mother hauled the arsenal from the home in a makeshift bag and discarded the contents into the nearby Wishkah River. Cobain later retrieved the weapons from the river, which were presumed lost by his mother and her boyfriend, and sold them to a local pawnshop. The proceeds were eventually put toward the purchase of an amplifier.

Despite her shortcomings, any criticism Cobain ever had toward his mother was brief. Furthermore, contrary to his limited relationship with his father, Cobain was always appreciative toward his mother and their communication remained routine. "My mother was a fantastic, attentive, and compassionate mother throughout my childhood, until I started becoming incorrigible and rebellious," he described to *Kerrang!* in 1993.

Cobain would eventually return to his father's home, albeit briefly, where the lost teenager was encouraged by his father to join the armed forces. A Naval recruiter met with Cobain at the family's home and, although the idea of stable housing and regular meals interested him, the teenager balked at the idea of enlistment. Soon after, he left his father's home once again.

As Cobain's housing issues persisted, a friend took notice. Jesse Reed had become one of Cobain's closest friends and his parents agreed to allow their son's friend to move in to their home. A religious family, the Reeds provided the teen with a nurturing environment in a large home several miles outside of Aberdeen. Unexpectedly for Cobain, he briefly gravitated toward religion while living with the Reeds and in October 1984 he was baptized at the family's church. For seven months, between 1984 and 1985, Cobain became a welcome presence in the Reeds' home and, once again, he felt like part of a genuine family dynamic. Despite his apparent growth, Cobain began to withdraw as his truancy and substance use continued. The Reeds' frustrations with Cobain culminated in the spring of 1985 when he was asked to move out after he broke a window to gain entry to the family's home after he forgot his key.

Cobain's housing instability, as legend now dictates, led to a brief period of homelessness which supposedly included residency under Aberdeen's Young Street Bridge, which crosses the Wishkah River. The tale was eventually immortalized in the Cobain penned "Something In the Way." The story's legitimacy is questionable due to the noisy overpass, diverse weather patterns, and varying river heights which often created muddy banks. Although some have contested the accuracy of his residency under the bridge and identify it as nothing more than a myth, locals and fans now regularly visit the bridge and have covered its underlying walls and pillars with graffiti in honor of Cobain.

At times, when housing options were minimal, Cobain would spend afternoons reading or sleeping at the Aberdeen Timberland Library and stay nights in the warm hallways of local apartment buildings. When all else failed, and he was left without a roof, Cobain walked to the Grays Harbor Community Hospital and slept in the lobby. With little motivation, Cobain also struggled to maintain regular employment, however brief janitorial and maintenance positions were acquired at J.M. Weatherwax High School, the local YMCA, and the Polynesian Hotel. In 1985, with no consistent source of income, Cobain was granted assistance and he began receiving $40 per month in food stamps. As someone with little appetite outside of sweets, he typically used portions of his assistance to trade for alcohol or marijuana. At the infancy of adulthood, residing in an economically and psychologically depressed region, and struggling with each passing day, Cobain's life was at risk of implosion. Eventually, the punk scene of the Pacific Northwest provided him an escape.

Although Cobain had played sports, largely to gain favor from his father, art remained his passion. His early artistic interests were channeled into visual arts, however he eventually turned to music as a source of solace as a pre-teen.

After beginning music classes in the fifth grade while attending the Montesano Junior High School, Cobain began playing drums in the school band two years later. He learned standard bass and snare patterns for basic songs which were rehearsed and randomly played at school assemblies and sporting events. He adored playing and sought to explore music further.

An introduction to the Beatles increased Cobain's interest and he quickly began to explore other musical artists. Initially a fan of pop, which included the Beatles and the Monkees, along with Arlo Guthrie's "Motorcycle Song" and Terry Jacks', "Seasons In the Sun," his musical interests eventually transitioned to 70s hard rock and new wave acts such as Black Sabbath, Led Zeppelin, Aerosmith, Queen, Kiss, Devo, and The B-52's. The lure of the famously cheap membership to the Columbia House record and tape club assisted with his exposure to new music and bands. Also, late at night and alone in his bedroom, Cobain listened to the Seattle radio station KISW through his headphones. Periodicals were typically stacked nearby, specifically *Rolling*

Stone and *Creem* magazines, which were filled with information he was unexposed to otherwise. He devoured whatever issues he had access to. One of Cobain's earliest introductions to punk rock was a detailed account of the Sex Pistols' 1978 American tour in an edition of *Creem*. His thirst was evident and some around him began to take notice.

Mari Earl, Cobain's maternal aunt, supported her nephew's increasing love of music by providing him with pop and rock records. Earl had also developed a love of music at a young age and began playing guitar when she was eleven. Her musicianship continued into adulthood with several local bands and for a short period of time she performed as a solo artist. Earl eventually gifted her nephew a bass drum and later a Hawaiian guitar along with an amplifier when he was eight years old. Their shared interest in music drew Cobain and his aunt together and she provided him with his first opportunities to make recordings. In an undated letter, printed in *Journals*, Cobain acknowledged the impact his aunt had on his introduction to music. "She also during those first precious years had given me the first three Beatles albums for which I am forever grateful knowing that my musical development would have probably come to a halt if I had to soak up one more year of the Carpenters and Olivia Newton John."

As his appetite to learn grew, Cobain received a Lindell guitar for his fourteenth birthday from his uncle, Chuck Fradenburg. Cobain's passion for the guitar was immediately clear to his uncle who then asked his friend, Warren Mason, to provide his nephew with lessons for $5 per half hour at the Rosevear Music Center in Aberdeen.

Although guitar lessons ended after just three months, reportedly at the insistence of Cobain's mother due to her son's further academic decline, he continued to practice at a feverish pace and began exploring the intricacies of songwriting and singing. He brought his guitar everywhere and quickly learned classics such as Led Zeppelin's "Stairway to Heaven," The Cars' "My Best Friend's Girl,"and AC/DC's "Back In Black." "As soon as I got my guitar, I just became so obsessed with it," Cobain recalled many years later. "And I stuck with it for so many years, every single night, for a few hours every day until I went to bed, I'd play my guitar. That's all I ever did. I always knew that I was doing something that was special," he continued. "I knew that I had something to offer, and I knew eventually I would have that opportunity to show people that I could write good songs, or I could at least contribute something musically."

Cobain spent countless hours in his room playing his guitar, occasionally at a thunderous volume resulting in irritated neighbors. His technique included playing with his left-hand on an inverted and restrung right-handed guitar, however at times he played with his right-hand and wrote with his left. Some suggested that this proved he was ambidextrous. The Lindell's condition was not perfect from the onset and Cobain was forced to learn simple methods to keep the instrument operational. The knowledge would serve him greatly in the future. As dynamics within his family remained unstable, Cobain turned to the guitar as a form of therapy, noting specifically in his journal that playing the guitar made him "less manically depressed."

In December 1982, while on Christmas break from school, Cobain traveled to his Aunt Mari's home, who had relocated to Burien, Washington, just south of Seattle. While visiting, Cobain used his aunt's recording equipment and made his first demo which he titled *Organized Confusion*. On the tape, Cobain played his guitar and used an empty overnight suitcase as a drum. In Nick Broomfield's *Kurt and Courtney*, Earl laughingly recounted Cobain's response, when he declined her offer to borrow a Roland Compu-Rhythm drum machine for a recording. "I want to keep my music pure," he replied. She later described the outcome of *Organized Confusion* as music drowned in distortion and heavy bass, however no complete tracks from the recording have ever surfaced.

Although punk music eventually piqued Cobain's musical interests further, his first concert experience was anything but punk. On March 29, 1983, he traveled to the Seattle Center Coliseum, along with friends and a six-pack of beer, to see Sammy Hagar and opening act Quarterflash. With few opportunities to explore music alternatives in Grays Harbor County, mainstream radio initially provided Cobain with his only exposure to musicians, such as "The Red Rocker." Even though Cobain purchased a Hagar T-shirt at the show, which he proudly wore to school soon after, he would eventually attempt to revise history and claim that Black Flag was his first concert.

Formed in 1976, Black Flag were considered pioneers of hardcore punk and a significant part of the punk subculture by the mid 80's. It was not until September 25,

1984, along with friends, that Cobain saw Black Flag during the band's *My War* tour at the Mountaineers in Seattle. He was reportedly forced to sell his record collection in order to purchase tickets to the show after his mother declined to provide any money for her son's punk rock interest. In addition to Cobain, members of the band the Melvins also attended the show.

In the summer of 1983, Cobain attended his first Melvins show in the parking lot behind a Thriftway located in Montesano, Washington. The Melvins had formed earlier the same year in Montesano and established a very small, but loyal fanbase among local teens. Otherwise, the band was heckled by the predominantly metal fanbase in Grays Harbor County. The Melvins unique combination of fast, aggressive, and loud rock n' roll was unlike anything locals had heard, including Cobain. He quickly developed a love for the band and began to regularly attend their rehearsals held behind their drummer's house in Aberdeen. After years of disregard from family and others, the teen had finally found a clique accepting of him. Cobain's relationship with the band members grew and he eventually worked sporadically as a roadie for the Melvins, and gained an education in the process, which would soon serve him well during his own eventual musical endeavors. In his journal Cobain recounted one of the first times he saw the Melvins perform live. "They played faster than I ever imagined music could be played and with more energy than my Iron Maiden records could provide. This was what I was looking for. Ah, punk rock. I came to the promised land of a grocery store parking lot and I found my special purpose." Emphasizing the impact of the experience, the sentence, "This was what I was looking for" was underlined in the passage.

Roger "Buzz" Osborne, singer and guitarist of the Melvins, befriended Cobain and introduced him to punk rock and hardcore music. Osborne made compilation tapes for Cobain which included bands he was not exposed to otherwise, such as Black Flag, Flipper, and MDC. Cobain adored the music which was introduced to him by Osborne and he devoured the tapes with a voracious appetite. It quickly became an irrevocable love. He cut his hair short and began to wear punk rock T-shirts. "I was always trying to find punk rock, but of course they didn't have it in our record shop in Aberdeen," Cobain later recalled. "Then finally Buzz Osborne, who had been a friend of mine off and on, made me a couple of compilation tapes and I was completely blown away. I'd finally found my calling. And I would lip sync to those tapes. I played them every day and it was the greatest thing. Punk expressed the way I felt socially and politically. There were so many things going on at once. It expressed the anger that I felt and the alienation. I found punk rock and it all came together."

2

A ROAD LESS TRAVELED

As a high school dropout with few prospects, Cobain's love of music offered hope in a relatively hopeless environment. Employment, housing, and even friendships were inconsistent, however music had not let him down. Cobain's abilities had grown as he continued to apply himself as a guitar player and a songwriter. Establishing a band was the natural next step. As such, in the fall of 1985, Cobain formed Fecal Matter; his first real band consisting of himself on vocals and guitar, the Melvins' drummer Dale Crover playing bass, and local Greg Hokanson playing drums. Soon after the inception of Fecal Matter, Hokanson was removed from the band for a variety of issues including his negative attitude.

For several months, Fecal Matter rehearsed original material written by Cobain, in addition to covers by Led Zeppelin and the Ramones. The band made plans to record and a logo for Fecal Matter was designed by Cobain. Featuring fresh feces with steam floating above, the logo was indicative of Cobain's lifelong fascination with all things related to the human body; a theme that would remain consistent in his art. Over a period of two days in early 1986, in what would become known as the earliest recorded examples of Cobain's songwriting, Fecal Matter recorded a crude demo Cobain titled *Illiteracy Will Prevail*. Featuring Cobain on guitar and vocals and Crover on bass and drums, the pair utilized Mari Earl's TEAC A-2340 four-track recorder during the sessions. Earl later recounted the recording process with Cobain biographer Charles Cross. "He (Cobain) arrived with a huge notebook full of lyrics. I showed him how to adjust a few things, how to record with reel-to-reel, and he went right at it."

Overall, thirteen songs were recorded during the sessions: "Sound of Dentage," "Bambi Slaughter," "Laminated Effect," "Control," "Downer," "Punk Rocker," "I Don't Want You," "Anorexorcist," "Accusations," "Spank Thru," "Insurance," "Class of '86," and "Blather's Log." "Spank Thru" became the only track from *Illiteracy Will Prevail* which eventually received an official release and a re-recorded version of "Downer" was later released on a future album. Copies of the demo were dubbed by Cobain and the cassette's J-card detailed the song titles and was illuminated with the band's logo, along with flies buzzing around for an added affect. As years passed, and Nirvana's popularity grew, *Illiteracy Will Prevail* became a highly sought after bootleg.

On May 3, 1986, a modified version of Fecal Matter called Brown Towel (misspelled as Brown Cow on posters) which included Cobain, Crover, and Osborne, had their only live performance to an audience of approximately twenty at the Greater Evergreen Students' Community Cooperative Organization in Olympia, Washington. Throughout the one-off show Cobain read poetry as Osborne and Crover backed him with a wall of distortion. Although the spoken word performance was not mind blowing, it became apparent to many that Cobain had talent and wasn't just a Melvins lackey. Later the same year, the group disbanded when the Melvins, which included Osborne and Crover, began supporting their debut EP, *Six Songs*. The album was released by Seattle-based C/Z Records and featured a photo of the Melvins taken by Krist Novoselic.

The son of Croatian immigrants, Kristo Novoselic and Marija Mustac, Krist Novoselic was born on May 16, 1965, in Compton, California. Raised speaking Croatian, Novoselic spent his early years in the Golden State before he and his family relocated to Aberdeen in 1979, largely to take advantage of employment opportunities and lower living expenses. His parents quickly acquired work in the small town, however Novoselic later recalled the drastic change he experienced at his new home. "It was a culture shock. Aberdeen was not only geographically isolated, it was culturally isolated. I missed the weather and the culture of California. Everybody in Aberdeen was listening to Kenny Rogers!"

Due to Novoselic's struggles acclimating to his new surroundings, in 1980 he was sent to reside with family for one year in Zadar, Croatia. While in Eastern Europe, Novoselic's interest in music grew as he discovered punk rock and new wave music via short wave radio from signals largely broadcast from the British Broadcasting Corporation. Soon after returning to Aberdeen, Novoselic was gifted a guitar and he began receiving lessons from Warren Mason, Cobain's future guitar instructor. Novoselic's prowess grew, along with his musical interests, and it quickly became evident to the teen that he had few commonalities with most of his peers in Aberdeen.

Cobain had noticed Novoselic, all of 6'7", two years prior when the pair walked the halls at J.M. Weatherwax High School. Although the pair shared no classes, Cobain found Novoselic to be clever and charismatic with a unique sense of humor. Additionally, contrary to Cobain's introverted nature, Novoselic was personable and, in subsequent years as their eventual friendship turned into a brotherhood, he spoke for the pair when necessary.

After graduating from high school in 1983, and as his love of music remained a common theme in his life, Novoselic established a relationship with Shelli Dilley; also a former student at J.M. Weatherwax High School. Despite the burgeoning relationship, Novoselic's life became stagnant as he transitioned from high school to various menial jobs in and around Aberdeen. It was during this time, while employed at Aberdeen's Taco Bell, that Novoselic was introduced by a co-worker to the Melvins' Buzz Osborne and Matt Lukin. Novoselic quickly developed a friendship with the pair and he soon became a regular during the Melvins' rehearsals along with other locals who were lovingly nicknamed by Osborne as the "Cling-Ons." Soon after, another local teen began attending the rehearsals named Kurt Cobain. Novoselic's brother, Robert Novoselic, introduced him to Cobain and a friendship developed. Like Cobain, Novoselic longed for an alternative in Aberdeen and found an escape in music, along with a fondness for the Melvins.

Hoping to form a new band following the dissolution of Fecal Matter, Cobain approached Novoselic with the offer and provided him with a copy of the *Illiteracy Will Prevail* demo. Despite Cobain's efforts, soon after Novoselic and his girlfriend relocated to Arizona to explore employment opportunities, however by the fall of 1986 the couple returned to Aberdeen. Though he was initially hesitant to accept Cobain's offer, Novoselic eventually listened to the demo upon his return and agreed to form a band and play bass. During their initial rehearsals, Cobain and Novoselic quickly established a half hour set encompassing new compositions and Fecal Matter songs, including "Downer" and "Spank Thru." The pair became close and discovered their commonalities which included shared musical interests and a disdain for many things related to Aberdeen.

In the fall of 1986, after securing a $200 loan from his mother, Cobain settled into a small house on East Second Street, along with Matt Lukin. The ramshackle structure, which was essentially rotting to the ground and often referred to by many as "the shack," quickly became a central hangout. It was a visible disaster with few amenities, however the condition of "the shack" quickly grew worse primarily due to Cobain's disregard toward any semblance of cleanliness and order. Aside from the debris that Cobain left behind in his wake, his pet turtles briefly occupied the only bathtub resulting in a foul smell that permeated throughout the already horrid home.

Eventual friction between the roommates was exacerbated when Cobain decided to tape a line of demarcation down the middle of "the shack," conveniently leaving the bathroom on his side. Lukin's frustrations were compounded further when the Melvins relocated to California and he was inexplicably replaced as the band's bass player. He would soon move out of "the shack," but quickly found stability as a co-founder of the pivotal Seattle band, Mudhoney. In need of financial support, Cobain allowed his friend, Dylan Carlson, to move in. He had met Carlson in early 1986 who, like Cobain, was mildly eccentric with unique ideological views. The pair remained close friends during the subsequent years and would eventually share many additional commonalities.

At nineteen, Cobain was on his own and reliant on no one. Income was minimal and a regimented employment schedule was inconsistent, however his focus on building a band was steadfast. In 1985, after receiving stitches on his finger from a cut caused by a piece of broken glass while he was employed briefly as a dishwasher, Cobain feared any job that might once again jeopardize his ability to play the guitar. He had little, however music was a necessity. By late 1986, Cobain's rehearsals with Novoselic were commonplace at "the shack" and briefly included Cobain on drums, while Novoselic played guitar, however the pair quickly transitioned back to what became routine throughout their career. Cobain later described their early sound as "totally abrasive;" a sound influenced by Black Sabbath, the Melvins, and Black Flag.

After recruiting fellow Aberdeen resident Bob McFadden on drums, Cobain and Novoselic christened their group as The Sellouts. Planned as a Creedence Clearwater

Revival tribute band, The Sellouts began rehearsals, but quickly ceased after approximately one month when McFadden left the project. The Sellouts lacked direction, a fact Cobain and Novoselic later acknowledged, and was only initially conceived as a bar band. Undeterred, in early 1987 Cobain and Novoselic recruited Aaron Burckhard as the band's new drummer, who the pair had met at the Melvins' rehearsals. After acquiring enough equipment, including used drum parts provided by Dale Crover, the trio immediately began to rehearse tracks from *Illiteracy Will Prevail* and write new material. Most nights were spent in similar fashion; repeatedly rehearsing songs, drinking, and smoking marijuana.

Cobain's musical prowess was immediately evident as he became the band's leader. At times, Cobain barely left "the shack" as he concentrated on songwriting and plotting next steps. "He was the lead songwriter," Novoselic recounted years later. "He had the idea - like he had riffs and a vocal line he'd be hammering out; he'd be holed up somewhere by himself, hammer things out, and then he would just start busting 'em out at rehearsal."

Along with his commitment to music, Cobain developed an increasing pattern of drug abuse while residing at "the shack." Most of his days were spent under the influence of any substance that was available, which at times included hallucinations and inhalants, in addition to old standards such as alcohol and marijuana. "He was totally into getting wasted, whatever the time of day. He was a real mess," Novoselic later recalled. It was likely not a coincidence that a stomach ailment, that would torment Cobain for years, also began at this time.

Though some would later dispute the timeline, in 1992 Cobain informed biographer Michael Azerrad that in 1986 he was introduced to opiates, which would later lead to heroin. After abusing the prescribed opiate Percodan excessively for days, which he had been obtained from the exploits of an acquaintance, Cobain's supply dried up resulting in his first drug withdrawal. The resulting sickness had no impact on his view of most drugs and by 1987 Cobain's struggle with addiction was becoming clear and would remain so throughout the rest of his short life. With evident and untreated mental health issues, largely attributed to the impact created by the trauma of his youth, Cobain's use of alcohol and drugs became a form of self-medication. Aside from music, substances were a means to cope. Long term co-occurring intervention to address both his mental health and substance abuse became necessary, but would never happen.

As a young man, Cobain struggled with the opposite sex largely due to his insecurities. In high school he was an outsider who had contrasting views and interests from a majority of the student body, resulting in alienation from many peers, including females. Cobain felt he was too skinny and he wore multiple layers of clothing to add to his physique, even during summer months. "I was a rodent like, underdeveloped, hyperactive spaz," he described in his journal. Some even presumed he was gay because of his physique and his friendships with classmates who were homosexual. As a result, few overtures were ever received from women or initiated by the teen.

Cobain met Tracy Marander, one year his senior, in 1986 after the pair began attending the same punk shows and parties. A resident of Olympia with a distinctive style and varying hair colors, Marander was unlike any of the women Cobain had become accustomed to in Aberdeen. He was instantly attracted to Marander and her interests, which included photography and a propensity for pets; cats, rabbits, turtles, and rats. More so than anything for Cobain, Marander was a veteran of dozens of local punk shows and was knowledgeable of the scene. Along with this, Marander was an early advocate of the Melvins. Ultimately, a flirtatious relationship, largely initiated by Marander, became sexual several months later. Their relationship quickly progressed and in June 1987, after twenty years in Grays Harbor County, Cobain moved into Marander's studio apartment in Olympia. Ironically, for a young man who had never had any consistent income, the apartment was located directly across the street from the Washington Lottery Headquarters. Cobain's move was completed in a single trip, with little more than his guitar, a small collection of records, and clothing stuffed carelessly into a single garbage bag. He later jokingly described the apartment as nothing more than a "shoebox," consisting of one bedroom, one bathroom, a small living room, and a closet sized kitchen. Almost immediately, Cobain gained an appreciation for the liberal city as the antithesis of Aberdeen, where his artistic talents were acknowledged and supported. Furthermore, providing Cobain with added comfort in the new environment, Marander's warm and supportive manner was something which had been largely inconsistent in his life for several years.

At times Cobain was unable to secure full time employment, however his desire for a regimented schedule was always minimal at best. Typically, he awoke at noon and rarely ventured outside the apartment, at times remaining inside for days. Along with completing art projects, an aesthetic which included diverse interpretations of the human body utilizing canvases, collages, doll parts, and clay, Cobain's days in Olympia were generally spent playing the guitar and watching an exorbitant amount of television. As a result, he was alone for hours in the couple's North Pear Street apartment while Marander worked a third shift position with Shelli Dilley at the Boeing airplane plant in Seattle. Most nights, while she was gone upwards of ten hours, Marander's expectations of Cobain were minimal and typically only included minor chores and the care of their numerous pets, however he became increasingly unreliable. "I am a totally pampered spoiled bum," Cobain acknowledged at the time in an unsent letter to Dale Crover. In an attempt to gain financial assistance, Marander urged Cobain to secure consistent employment, however he would just threaten to move out or sleep in the car. Any frustration Marander had was typically brief and she regularly left notes for Cobain to find during her absence offering him encouraging words and professing her love. Over time, Marander became witness to Cobain's burgeoning musical talent, whether he strummed his guitar while watching television or whispered lyrics to himself. The privacy and motherly support he was afforded by Marander allowed Cobain to focus on his art and songwriting; the latter of which flourished profoundly during the course of the couple's relationship.

On Saturday, March 7, 1987, after a previous show in Olympia fell through days prior, the young band performing as Skid Row and consisting of Cobain, Novoselic, and Burckhard, made their live debut at a house party in Raymond, Washington. The show had been arranged by Ryan Aigner, a former J.M. Weatherwax student and a frequent spectator during the band's early rehearsals, who had briefly taken on a managerial role. Using his work van from Benny's Quality Floors, Aigner drove the band and their equipment, along with Tracy Marander and Shelli Dilley, approximately twenty-five miles south of Aberdeen to Raymond. Once the trek was complete, the house was located down a gravel road, on the outskirts of the remote town. Following their arrival, tension was evident as it became clear the rag tag group were unlike a majority of the partygoers. Regardless, the band was undeterred and slowly set up their equipment in the living room area of the house for the unpaid gig.

After warming up with "Downer," the band transitioned into an approximate six minute rendition of "Aero Zeppelin" which received a lackadaisical response from the mingling audience who, unsurprisingly, were focused on alcohol. Despite some eventual minor heckling from the audience, Cobain's intensity was evident in Raymond, as much as it would be at any theatre or festival show in later years, as he stared ahead, hair slightly blinding his vision, and singing with abandon. Cobain felt a sense of delight in "freaking out the rednecks" during their raucous set which also included performances of "If You Must, "Mexican Seafood," "Pen Cap Chew," "Spank Thru," and "Hairspray Queen," and was recorded by an acquaintance using a Sony Walkman and later widely bootlegged.

As the show progressed, Cobain and Novoselic became intoxicated and began jumping off tables. "We had everyone so scared of us that they were in the kitchen hiding from us," Cobain later recalled. Novoselic then took off his shirt and covered himself with fake blood, which had been left about randomly from Halloween several months prior, while Marander and Dilley groped his chest and kissed each other in an orgiastic scene that alarmed many, but thrilled Cobain.

The band played for nearly one hour and, despite the likely annoyance of the partygoers, out of eight songs and several jams, their set consisted solely of originals with the exception of Led Zeppelin's "Heartbreaker." Eventually, the group was asked to leave when Novoselic, whose inhibitions were impacted by a night of continuous drinking, went outside and began to urinate on various cars. Piling back into Aigner's van, along with the band's equipment and seated lopsided on rolls of carpet, the group then fled into the night. Taking into account the punk ethos which the band valued, after shocking the partygoers and receiving little zeal during their raucous performance, they considered the show a success.

As their enthusiasm grew following the Raymond performance, the band took the stage next on April 18, 1987, at the Community World Theater, located in Tacoma, Washington. With assistance from Cobain's girlfriend who knew the venue's booker, Jim May, the band secured a regular slot at the somewhat dilapidated former adult movie theater. Attendance was sparse at the initial theater shows and although they were barely paid at times, the band gained confidence and a small fanbase. Over the course of a year, regular shows at the Community World Theater provided the band with freedom to grow as musicians while preparing material for their first album. By all accounts, the band would have continued to play at the Community World Theater into the future, however the theater closed in June 1988.

Less than two months following their debut in Raymond, and still performing as Skid Row, the band played their fourth official set in public on KAOS radio, located on the campus of the progressive Evergreen State College, in Olympia, Washington. The recorded appearance aired on two overlapping programs, "Out of Order" and "Toy Train Crash Backside Bone Beefcake," and became the band's first demo. During the appearance the set included performances of "Love Buzz," "Floyd the Barber," "Downer," "Spank Thru," "Mexican Seafood," and "Hairspray Queen."

Along with Cobain, Novoselic also relocated south of Aberdeen which made rehearsals with Burckhard difficult. Despite the logistics, the band was initially able to gather somewhat regularly at the insistence of Cobain whose fervor was unmatched. At times, Cobain expected the band to rehearse every day for hours. Unfortunately, Burckhard's propensity for volatility and his lack of commitment, which included a pattern of absences from scheduled rehearsals, contributed to strain within the band. He felt the band was nothing more than a hobby and would not result in financial reward. Ultimately, Burckhard resigned due to a work obligation as the nighttime assistant manager at Burger King in Aberdeen.

In October 1987, following a brief lapse in productivity throughout the summer of 1987 due to Burckhard's departure and Novoselic's own commitment to two jobs, Cobain and Novoselic reunited. The pair built a rehearsal space in the basement of Novoselic's residence, whose focus on the band had sharpened, and an ad was placed for a new drummer in *The Rocket*, a Seattle-based music newspaper: "SERIOUS DRUMMER WANTED. Underground attitude, Black Flag, Melvins, Zeppelin, Scratch Acid, Ethel Merman. Versatile as heck. Kurdt 352-0992." Cobain's respelling of his first name was used intermittently during the band's early days before he reverted back to the traditional spelling for the remainder of his career. Rationale for the brief change was never explained. Although the ad did not receive any responses, Cobain and Novoselic continued to rehearse whenever possible. Eventually, with no suitable replacement, the Melvins' Dale Crover agreed to fill in briefly for the departed Burckhard.

For months the band went through a series of names, including Throat Oyster, Pen Cap Chew, Windowpane, Ted Ed Fred, Bliss, and the aforementioned Skid Row, before settling on Nirvana in 1988. Cobain's brief interest in Buddhism contributed to the name which appeared in public for the first time on a flyer for a show at the Community World Theatre on March 19, 1988. According to Cobain, "I wanted a name that was kind of beautiful or nice and pretty instead of a mean, raunchy punk name like the Angry Samoans." As defined by Webster's, Nirvana is "the extinction of desire, passion, illusion, and the empirical self and attainment of rest, truth, and unchanging being."

3

RECIPROCAL RECORDING

Originally founded in January 1984 by Chris Hanzsek and Tina Casale, Reciprocal Recording was in need of a new studio by 1985 after losing the lease on their original space located in an office suite in Seattle's Interbay neighborhood. In 1986, with assistance from Jack Endino, a Seattle based producer and a guitarist in the band Skin Yard, Reciprocal Recording secured a new space in a small unassuming triangular building located in the city's Ballard neighborhood. Following its original construction in the early 20th century, the building was used in several ways before a period of vacancy in the early 1970s. In 1976, the building was repurposed as Triangle Recording and used as a production space by bands of various genres before eventually transitioning to what would become Reciprocal Recording; a renowned studio in the thriving Seattle music scene. Once interior construction was completed and Reciprocal Recording opened in June 1986, the windowless studio appeared small and unique, but was a "funky space," according to journalist Michael Azerrad. Despite the uniqueness of the space, its sound quality offered little more than what could be accomplished by a good producer within a basement. Endino later described Reciprocal Recording as "a terrible studio," but acknowledged further, "I had nothing to compare it to." Regardless, as an inexpensive studio with good equipment, it enticed many bands in the Seattle region.

Although Endino was initially viewed as a partner at Reciprocal Recording after the studio relocated to the Ballard neighborhood, the arrangement was brief and he chose to instead be an independent producer, free of any obligations to the studio. Endino's relationships within the Seattle scene led to many recordings at Reciprocal Recording by bands who used the studio in the infancy of their careers; dozens recorded by Endino himself. "For a year, it seemed like every single band was coming to me," Endino would later recall. "Maybe they trusted me because I was a musician." A musician at heart, Endino was reluctant to refer to himself as a producer on early records. Instead, he was credited with the term "recorded by." Notable albums recorded by Endino, inside the approximate 900-square-foot space with the studio's vintage equipment, included Green River's *Dry As a Bone* EP in 1986, Soundgarden's debut EP *Screaming Life* in 1987, Mudhoney's debut EP *Superfuzz Bigmuff* in 1988, and TAD's debut LP *God's Balls* in 1989.

Sadly, despite its short and successful history, Reciprocal Recording closed in August of 1991. Although the studio had closed, the space has continued to be used as a recording studio, now known as Hall of Justice, and is recognized regionally as a historical landmark.

One afternoon, Endino fielded an unsolicited call from Cobain. "We just got a phone call at the studio one day from this guy, you know, Kurt, says his name was Kurt, he said he was a friend of the Melvins," Endino later recalled. "He wanted to come up and just record some songs. And I said, 'Ok, friend of the Melvins, friend of mine. Come on up.' You know I didn't know who the hell he was and nobody else did either." Cobain noted that the Melvins' Dale Crover would be sitting in on drums during the session, albeit as a brief addition, and Endino's interest was piqued further. The band's initial session was booked for six hours at a rate of $20 per hour and misspelled by Endino in Reciprocal Recording's scheduling log under the name "Kurt Covain." Cobain was attracted to Reciprocal Recording's cheap rate after he saw an ad in *The Rocket*. Crover would later recall that Cobain wanted to record at Reciprocal Recording because he liked the sound of Soundgarden's *Screaming Life* EP released three months prior. Soon after his call to Endino, Cobain and the band piled their equipment into a friend's distinctive Chevy camper van, which was covered in shingles and heated with a wood stove, and set out from Olympia to Seattle.

On January 23, 1988, shortly before noon, a band not yet christened as Nirvana, but rather Ted Ed Fred, entered Reciprocal Recording for the first time. Michael Azzerad described Reciprocal Recording as a place where "the paint peeled off the particle board walls, there were cigarette burns all over every horizontal surface, and it didn't matter a bit if you spilled your beer on the floor." Despite the surroundings, the band members were inspired by the opportunity before them and blind to the conditions of the studio.

Committed to six hours at Reciprocal Recording, the band members were thoroughly focused on having an efficient session due to the lack of supplemental funds and a gig commitment arranged by Crover that night forty miles away at the Community World Theater. Following initial introductions with Endino, there were few additional pleasantries and the band quickly set up their equipment and laid down instrumental tracks, beginning with "If You Must." After Novoselic finished tracking his parts, he smoked marijuana, and went to wait in the camper where a fresh fire had been lit to tackle the wintry conditions. Later, Cobain laid down the vocals and by 4:00 P.M. the band had concluded the recording process and in most cases only one take of each song was completed.

Overall, ten songs were recorded during the session: "If You Must," "Downer," "Floyd the Barber," "Paper Cuts," "Spank Thru," "Hairspray Queen," "Aero Zeppelin," "Beeswax," "Mexican Seafood," and "Pen Cap Chew." The band also hoped to record "Anorexorcist" and "Raunchola" during the session, however they ran out of time. The two tracks were eventually dropped from future plans and never recorded. Upon completion, the six hour session cost the band $152.44 and was paid for by Cobain using money he had earned from a brief position as a janitor at Lemon Janitorial. The session proved to be successful in many ways and three of the ten recordings were eventually used on Nirvana's first album: "Floyd the Barber," "Paper Cuts," and "Downer." Although the group was inexperienced, the process of recording and mixing ten songs went smoothly. "(It) went by so fast that I barely remember even talking with them," Endino later recalled. "It was one of the fastest sessions I had ever done." A rough mix of the session, later referred to as the *Dale Demo*, was completed by Endino once recording had concluded. After packing up their equipment, the band was provided a cassette copy of the session by Endino as they quickly left Reciprocal Recording. Gazing at the finished tape, Cobain's dream was becoming a realization and, while they drove south along Interstate 5 toward their gig commitment in Tacoma, the band listened to the demo twice as the camper's excessive weight caused it to drag along random imperfections in the roadway.

Following the band's departure, Endino made his own mix from the eight-track master, which the band reluctantly left behind at Endino's request. His decision to record his own copy was not unique, but something about the trio stood out to Endino. He sent a copy of the *Dale Demo* and Cobain's phone number to Jonathan Poneman, the co-founder of the Seattle based record label Sub Pop. He also sent copies of the demo to Shirley Carlson of the Seattle radio station KCMU and to writer Dawn Anderson of *Backlash*. Endino's decision would ultimately provide the band with radio airplay and an eventual record contract.

Poneman later recalled his conversation with Endino following the session: "He told me, 'There's this kid who came in who looks like a car mechanic. He came up with Dale Crover. He lives in Olympia and his name is Kurt. To be honest, I don't even really know what to make of this tape. It's awesome, but they just bashed it out and it's unlike anything I've really heard. The guy's got an amazing voice.'" Poneman also became an advocate for the band and was particularly fond of track one, "If You Must." His fondness of the song was unknown to Cobain who disliked the song himself which was soon dropped from the band's repertoire.

The day following Nirvana's recording session, the *Dale Demo* began to make the rounds in Seattle. Enlivened by the session, Cobain sent copies to friends and unsolicited copies were sent to various indie labels, along with handwritten letters. He did not receive any responses from the labels and, although the *Dale Demo* did not lead to an immediate change for the band, "Floyd the Barber" was soon in regular rotation on KCMU. "Floyd the Barber," one of Nirvana's first finished songs and a staple in their early live shows, was interpreted as a psychotic reimagination of characters featured on *The Andy Griffith Show* and built around bleakness and sarcasm like several other early songs by the band.

In March 1988, Crover moved to San Francisco to return to his responsibilities with the Melvins and once again Nirvana was without a drummer. Soon after, at the recommendation of Crover, drums were filled by Dave Foster. Like Cobain and Novoselic until just months prior, Foster was a resident of Aberdeen. Otherwise, the pair shared few additional commonalities with Foster, who had a mustache, short hair, and a somewhat aggressive demeanor, but his drumming was needed by the band. Regardless, Foster's position as Nirvana's drummer was brief after he was incarcerated for two weeks following a physical altercation with the mayor's son of the nearby town of Cosmopolis. As an additional consequence of the arrest, Foster lost his license and was subsequently unable to attend rehearsals. Aaron Burckhard then briefly rejoined the band, but within a few days he was arrested for driving while intoxicated. Subtly,

Foster and Burckhard were relieved of their duties with the band while Cobain and Novoselic sought a fresh start.

Once again, Cobain and Novoselic placed an ad in *The Rocket* in order to find a new drummer: "DRUMMER WANTED. Play hard, sometimes light, underground, versatile, fast, medium slow, versatile, serious, heavy, versatile, dorky, nirvana, hungry. Kurdt 352-0992." The ad did not receive any responses, however the pair had developed interest in a drummer known from local shows named Chad Channing.

Just three weeks older than Cobain, Chad Channing had been a veteran of several regional bands by the spring of 1988. As an avid soccer player whose hero was Pelé, at the age of thirteen Channing shattered his left femur in a freak accident during gym class which required eight surgeries and five years of rehabilitation. Largely immobile at times during his recovery and unable to return to the pitch, Channing's parents hoped to boost their son's spirit with music. He began playing bass guitar to pass the time, along with other instruments. "He seemed delighted and within a couple of weeks we could hear guitar riffs that we thought were coming from a Van Halen record. He was incredible," his parents later recalled. It became clear that Channing possessed musical ability and, once his leg began to heal and casts had been permanently removed, his parents bought him a used drum set. "The first time I sat behind a kit putting out rhythm wasn't a struggle at all," Channing later recalled. "It made totally perfect sense." The instrument provided Channing the ability to attain further depth to his musicianship while also helping his injured leg gain strength. Particularly fascinated by the drumming abilities of Led Zeppelin's John Bonham, Channing spent countless hours in his bedroom with headphones on and playing along to numerous Led Zeppelin songs. He eventually discovered punk rock with the assistance of his former classmate and friend, Ben Shepherd. With little hope of graduating from high school prior to his twentieth birthday, due to the numerous absences accumulated as a result of his injury and recovery, Channing chose to withdraw and pursue a career in music.

Despite his small 5'6" stature, Channing played powerfully behind a large North kit which was unlike many used by drummers throughout the local scene. After hearing Channing's style with his previous band, Tic Dolly Row, Cobain and Novoselic were intrigued. The drummer was eventually approached by the pair at the Community World Theater on May 6, 1988, during Malfunkshun's farewell performance, where he was invited to rehearse with the band. Although Channing did not initially join the band, Cobain and Novoselic were persistent and one rehearsal led to another until he played his first show with Nirvana before a sparse audience in late May 1988. "They never actually said, 'okay you're in,'" Channing later acknowledged.

In an effort to conform to the simple presentation Cobain and Novoselic valued, Channing stripped his large kit down to the basics. Rehearsals initially took place in the basement of Novoselic's rented home in Tacoma and later transitioned to a space above Novoselic's mother's hair salon in Aberdeen; Maria's Hair Design. The change occurred after

Novoselic and his girlfriend briefly separated and he was forced to move back to Aberdeen. As a resident of Bainbridge Island, Channing had never been to Aberdeen prior to meeting Novoselic and Cobain. His first impression was one of alarm. "It was really bad," he later recalled. "It's probably the poorest section in all of Washington. All of a sudden you have this instant slum."

Channing's drumming ability and relaxed demeanor finally provided Nirvana with the prospect of long term stability and the trio quickly transitioned into a schedule of routine rehearsals. Essentially, with the addition of Channing, the first official incarnation of Nirvana was born.

4

SUB POP

In 1971, Evergreen State College opened in Olympia. The progressive school was unlike most at the time and allowed students to fashion their own academic experience while receiving evaluations from teachers, not grades. Raised in Illinois, Bruce Pavitt transferred from Blackburn College to Evergreen College in 1979. Shortly following his arrival, Pavitt began volunteering at the college's radio station, KAOS. Like the college, the station was unique largely due to the steadfast vision of the music director, John Foster, who ensured that eighty percent of the music broadcast had to originate from independent labels. Pavitt was amazed by the station's vast music library which encompassed rare albums by independent bands from throughout the United States. "I hung out at the KAOS library, studied their records and got college credit for it," Pavitt later noted. An idea occurred to Pavitt: How would most people discover that any of this music existed or know how to access it?

Subterranean Pop, a fanzine by Pavitt designed to expose the American independent music scene, released its first issue in May 1980. The fanzine took its name from Pavitt's radio show, "Subterranean Pop," broadcast on KAOS. Issues featured reports on various scenes throughout the country and album reviews, along with contact information which provided readers the ability to order albums that would be inaccessible elsewhere.

Following the release of the third issue in 1982, the fanzine title was shortened to simply *Sub Pop* and then, beginning with the fifth issue, Pavitt began randomly releasing cassette compilations along with issues. Pavitt wrote in the fourth issue, "Cassettes are the ultimate tool. Unlike records, production and manufacturing can happen-within minutes-in your own living room!" The cassettes featured tracks from independent bands from around the country and the J-cards were illustrated by artists attending Evergreen State College. In 1986, due to the cassettes' moderate success, *Sub Pop* transitioned into a record label with the release of its first vinyl LP, *Sub Pop 100*; a compilation featuring tracks by the U-Men, Sonic Youth, Scratch Acid, and Skinny Puppy. The album eventually sold 5,000 copies which substantiated the release of future albums by Sub Pop.

After introducing the pair in 1986, Soundgarden's Kim Thayil urged Pavitt and Jonathan Poneman to explore a partnership. It quickly became evident that the pair shared similar musical interests and aspirations. A musician and a radio host on KCMU, Poneman had motivation and confidence, but also finances. Following the release of *Sub Pop 100*, though a customer base was evident, Sub Pop lacked sufficient financing to proceed with additional productions and distribution. As a result, in 1987, Poneman agreed to invest $19,000 in the label and, in exchange, he became partners with Pavitt. Due to the ripe scene in Seattle, which was seemingly overflowing with talent as evidenced by *Sub*

Pop 100 and the *Deep Six* compilation produced in 1986 by Chris Hanzsek and Tina Casale on C/Z Records, the pair saw opportunity with the label and hoped to make it synonymous with the Pacific Northwest. "Focus on the Northwest, be a Northwest record label, the same as Motown was a Detroit label," Pavitt later recalled.

In June 1987, Sub Pop released Soundgarden's "Hunted Down" / "Nothing to Say" single and Green River's debut *Dry As a Bone* EP; the latter a release that had initially been delayed for one year due to Sub Pop's financial difficulties. Ultimately, in just the first few years of its existence, Sub Pop would release albums by several regional standouts, including Soundgarden, Mudhoney, Screaming Trees, Green River, and TAD, subsequently establishing itself as an independent powerhouse. Though the term "grunge" had been used as a genre reference before, it was Sub Pop's catalogue description of *Dry As a Bone* as "ultra loose grunge that destroyed the morals of a generation," that contributed further to the eventual genre defining term.

The following year, with the slogan "We're ripping you off big time," Sub Pop established the innovative Sub Pop Singles Club - a subscription service which afforded subscribers the opportunity to receive a seven inch vinyl single by mail from the label on a monthly basis. Costing $35 for a one year subscription, or $20 for six months, the Sub Pop Singles Club was conceived largely to provide the young label with a steady source of income at a necessary time. "We were making far more commitments than we could afford," Poneman recounted in Greg Prato's *Grunge Is Dead*. "The one way people could ensure that they would get a single and we would have cash flow was to have people pay up front."

Over the course of several months Cobain continued to mail numerous unsolicited tapes and letters to many independent labels in an attempt to promote Nirvana, including indie powerhouses SST (Black Flag, Meat Puppets, Husker Du), Alternative Tentacles (Dead Kennedys), and Touch and Go (Big Black, Scratch Acid), however he never received a single reply. "Do you think you could please send us a reply of fuck off or not interested so we don't have to waste more money sending more tapes," Cobain begged in one letter.

Over time Sub Pop expressed interest in Nirvana, largely due to Endino's adulation, and on April 10, 1988, Pavitt and Poneman traveled to the Central Tavern in Seattle and planned to be in attendance for the band's scheduled show. Prior to April 10, the band had performed less than two dozen shows during their young career, but their confidence and ability were increasing exponentially. Unfortunately, in what was perhaps their most important performance to date, other than the band, their girlfriends, and the label bosses, the club was all but empty. Embarrassed by the scene, the band quickly packed their gear and left. Although the band presumed fallout from the Central Tavern disaster was inevitable, Pavitt and Poneman saw potential in Nirvana and the band was offered a booking on April 24, 1988, at the Vogue to support Blood Circus as part of "Sub Pop Sunday." Although Cobain was disappointed with the band's performance, which had occurred in front of roughly twenty attendees, soon after "Sub Pop Sunday" Poneman sought to coordinate a meeting with Cobain and Novoselic at the Cafe Roma coffeehouse. "I was in awe of Kurt's talents," Poneman later acknowledged in Everett True's *Nirvana: The Biography*. "Also, I had to lure my Sub Pop crew to seeing the light about Nirvana. So any reluctance was just the art of hem-and-haw until folks felt comfortable."

Gathered around a table in the relaxed setting of the coffeehouse, Cobain barely said a word and Novoselic neared intoxication from a smuggled beverage, however the label bosses earnestly offered the band a recording deal. Contrary to Cobain's hope, Sub Pop did not want to release an original composition, but rather a single containing the band's cover version of "Love Buzz." The original version of "Love Buzz," released by the Shocking Blue in 1969 on their album titled *At Home*, had been discovered by Novoselic some time before while he thumbed through a one dollar bin at Dill's Second Hand Store, located in Aberdeen. Both Cobain and Novoselic embraced the Dutch band's song and a cover version by Nirvana quickly became a standard part of their live shows. A handshake agreement with Pavitt and Poneman concluded the meeting and soon after plans were made for the band to enter the studio. The agreement was also a bonus for Channing, who had seemingly joined the band just weeks prior.

The plan for "Love Buzz" frustrated Cobain, specifically because the band's first release would be a cover and the single would not be available in stores. Regardless of the band's position, Sub Pop would be financing the recording and there had been no interest expressed from any other labels. Although Pavitt did eventually ask Cobain if the band could front the cost for the recording, an act that infuriated the band and those in their circle, the label reconsidered and a session was booked soon after.

On June 11, 1988, Nirvana returned to Reciprocal Recording to record a cover of "Love Buzz." During the session, in addition to "Love Buzz," the band recorded the Cobain penned "Big Cheese," "Blandest," and re-recorded "Spank Thru," the latter which had originally been recorded by Fecal Matter on *Illiteracy Will Prevail* and later by Nirvana on the *Dale Demo*. Because the "Love Buzz" session took longer than expected, on June 30, 1988, the band returned to Reciprocal Recording in order to finish recording "Big Cheese."

Coinciding with the forthcoming release of the band's single, the first article ever written on Nirvana was published in the August 1988 issue of *Backlash*. During Cobain's interview with the article's author, Dawn Anderson, he detailed his history with the Melvins while noting that he hoped Nirvana did not sound like a "Melvins rip-off." According to the prophetic writer, "The group's way ahead of most mortals in the songwriting department and, at risk of sounding blasphemous, I honestly believe that with enough practice, Nirvana could become...better than the Melvins."

In November 1988, the "Love Buzz" / "Big Cheese" single became the Sub Pop Singles Club's first release. The single was limited to 1,000 numbered copies, with an additional 200 copies identified with a red slash instead of a number. The Sub Pop catalogue described the "Love Buzz" single as "heavy pop sludge from these untamed drop-ins." Although Nirvana initially intended to release "Blandest" as the B-side to "Love Buzz," the band eventually settled on "Big Cheese;" a song that reportedly acted as a sarcastic reference to Sub Pop co-founder, Jonathan Poneman.

The band members kept nearly 100 copies of the single for themselves for promotion and distribution to family members and friends. Two years prior, as Cobain and Novoselic worked to build the band, Novoselic's father would express to the boys, "Why don't you trade those guitars for shovels?" As an acknowledgement to Kristo Novoselic, the remark was imprinted near the outside of the groove on the single's A-side.

The front and back covers of the "Love Buzz" single featured photographs of the band taken by Alice Wheeler at "Never Never Land" located at the Point Defiance Park near the Tacoma Narrows Bridge. She and legendary Seattle photographer Charles Peterson were friends, and both were friends with Sub Pop co-founders Pavitt and Poneman. According to Wheeler, Peterson was given the job to photograph Mudhoney, and not Nirvana, because Sup Pop presumed they would be the bigger stars. She was paid $25 by Sub Pop for what became her first paid job as a photographer. The resulting single has become a rare artifact from the infancy of a legendary band, typically reselling for thousands of dollars.

According to a review of the "Love Buzz" single by the *Melody Maker's* Everett True, "Nirvana are beauty incarnate. A relentless two-chord garage beat which lays down some serious foundations for a sheer monster of a guitar force to howl over. The volume control ain't been built yet which can do justice to this three-piece." True also made the "Love Buzz" the U.S. single of the week describing it as "Limited edition of 1,000; love songs for the psychotically disturbed."

As Sub Pop gained interest in recording an album with Nirvana, Cobain continued to distribute unsolicited tapes to prospective labels. He described the band's sound as "Black Sabbath playing the Knack, Black Flag, Led Zeppelin, and the Stooges, with a pinch of the Bay City Rollers." One tape compiled by Cobain was titled *Kurt's Kassette*. With more material available than ever before, tapes included songs from the *Dale Demo* and the "Love Buzz" sessions, in addition to home recordings made by Cobain, including an extended sound collage titled "Montage of Heck." In an attempt to further publicize the band, Cobain delivered the "Love Buzz" / "Big Cheese" single to KCMU himself. Upon his arrival, Cobain met with the station manager and described "Love Buzz" as "a beautifully soft and mellow, crooning, sleep jingle." Soon after leaving the station, while disguising his voice, Cobain proceeded to phone in a request to KCMU for the single to be played. Twenty minutes later, as he and his girlfriend drove cautiously within range of the station for fear that the signal would be lost, "Love Buzz" was played over the airwaves. Tracy Marander later recalled that Cobain had "a big smile on his face" as the single was played.

5

BLEACH

As Nirvana began to receive accolades following the release of the "Love Buzz / Big Cheese" single, a natural progression with Sub Pop was assumed. To prepare, Cobain borrowed *All You Need To Know About the Music Business* from the library, however the band's future with the cash strapped label remained unclear even as preparations were being made to record their first studio album.

After an intoxicated Novoselic reportedly arrived at Bruce Pavitt's home in December demanding a contract for the band, Sub Pop offered Nirvana an extended contract with the label. The rudimentary fill- in-the-blank two page contract detailed an initial one-year agreement beginning on January 1 and ending on December 31, 1989, with options for two subsequent years through 1991. The contract specified a $600 advance for the band during the initial year, essentially a reimbursement for the recording of their debut, with a $12,000 advance for their first option year and a $24,000 advance for the second option year. Notably, the contract demanded three complete album length master tapes, requiring one for the initial year and one for each of the option years. With the signatures of each band member on

June 3, 1989, Nirvana became the first band to sign an extended contract with Sub Pop.

In December 1988, prior to securing a contract with Sub Pop, Nirvana began a series of rehearsals in preparation for their first album resulting in several new tracks. Rehearsals continued at Maria's Hair Design and typically began in the late evening after the business closed and continued into the early morning hours. Preparation for rehearsal days created difficulties largely due to the distance between all band members. For months, Novoselic would travel two hundred miles in his van before the band played a single note; Tacoma to Olympia to pick up Cobain, Olympia to Seattle (where the Bainbridge Island ferry docked) to pick up Channing, and Seattle to Aberdeen. Then, after typically practicing for several hours, Novoselic would drive everyone home.

Midday on Christmas Eve, 1988, recording began at Reciprocal Recording for what would become Nirvana's first album. "We had nothing else to do," Novoselic later recalled jokingly. Once again, Jack Endino would be mastering the controls during the recording process. The band was prepared and knew what sound they hoped to get on tape, a sound that Endino later described as "a dry, crunchy, 70s-rock sound." Overall, the sessions were spread across six days, during a one month period, and totaled approximately thirty hours (December 24, December 29-31, 1988 and January 14 and January 24, 1989) on an eight-track - four tracks for the drums, track five for bass, track six for guitars, track seven for vocal doubling or harmonies, and track eight for vocals - and concluded on January 24, 1989. There were few outtakes from the sessions largely to avoid the need to purchase additional tapes; an expense no one could afford. If a take wasn't good enough it was simply recorded over. Endino was impressed with the band's focus during the recording process and later stated, "They were very much about the music at the time, absolutely focused on what they were doing which they had to be very efficient to be able to make recordings that quickly and that good."

Although Sub Pop had initially requested an EP from Nirvana, the band had enough material to record a full length album utilizing both old and new compositions, including previously recorded tracks "Floyd the Barber," "Love Buzz," and "Paper Cuts." Cobain's new compositions prepared for the sessions included "About a Girl," one of the most unabashed pop songs he would ever write. He reportedly listened to the Fab Four's debut album, *Meet the Beatles*, all afternoon before writing the song. The track was a partial acknowledgment to his girlfriend, Tracy Marander, after she asked why he never wrote any songs about her. Soon after it was written, but still without a title, Channing asked Cobain "What is that song about?" He said "about a girl" to which Channing stated "Why don't you just call it that?" Channing later recounted that Cobain looked up with a quirky smile and stated simply, "Ok." "School" consisted of just two lines lyrically and fifteen words overall, but is a perfect example of Nirvana's early sound while also hinting at the dynamics that would become their second album. The song was a clear reference to high school and how its absurdity carries over to adulthood; cliques and snobs - "You're in high school again!" Contrary to the pop sensibilities of "About a Girl," "Negative Creep" was a ferocious two-note juggernaut, but was reportedly a rush job. Some viewed the song as Cobain's autobiographical reference to himself as a negative person and the chorus lyric "stoned" referring to his drug use in high school. Other new tracks highlighted Aberdeen stereotypes, such as "Swap Meet" and "Mr. Moustache."

In many interviews Cobain routinely disregarded the importance of lyrics, however some critics would contend that lyrics were just as important to the lead singer as the music. In 1993, during an interview with *Spin* magazine, Cobain recalled how he rushed through the lyrics for most of the band's first album the night before initial recordings began. "Let's just scream negative lyrics, and as long as they're not sexist and don't get too embarrassing it'll be ok," he recalled at the time. Despite his supposed lackadaisical approach to lyrics, Cobain described his methods toward lyricism in the same interview as collages of previously written pieces of poetry. "I picked out good lines, cut up things. I'm always skipping back and forth to different themes." Also, he detailed in a journal entry, "My lyrics are a big pile of contradictions," and "I like to be passionate and sincere, but I also like to have fun and act like a dork." Now, with the benefit of hindsight, what can be presumed is that Cobain was calculated and released nothing without careful consideration of not only the band's sound, but also his own reputation within the scene. Novoselic would later describe, "And so he was also very careful about and stubborn about how the way the art and the work was presented, because he didn't want to be humiliated."

Eleven tracks were selected for the album: "Blew," "Floyd the Barber," "About a Girl," "School," "Love Buzz,"

"Paper Cuts," "Negative Creep," "Scoff," "Swap Meet," "Mr. Moustache," and "Sifting." Beginning with Novoselic's throbbing bass on "Blew," styles on the album were interspersed and included pop, sludge, punk, and metal. Along with various styles, strong hooks were present and would be refined by the band over the course of the next two years in spectacular fashion. "Floyd the Barber," "Paper Cuts," and "Downer," which had been completed with Dale Crover at Reciprocal Recording in January 1988, were remixed and not re-recorded with Channing. A reissue of the album, released by Sub Pop in 1992 following the success of Nirvana's second album, included the tracks "Big Cheese" and "Downer." A recording of "Big Long Now," which was completed during the sessions, was not included on the album, but was eventually released on the band's 1992 compilation, *Incesticide*.

Following the editing and sequencing of the album, Bruce Pavitt felt that it should be entirely resequenced by Endino prior to release. Initially Cobain and Novoselic hoped for "Floyd the Barber" to open the album, however Pavitt's overruling led to "Blew" as the first track. Additionally, the release was delayed from March to June in order for Sub Pop to secure sufficient funds to distribute the album.

Although the album's working title was *Too Many Humans*, Cobain became inspired by an AIDS prevention poster he observed while the band drove around San Francisco in February 1989. The poster featured the phrase "bleach your works" as a reference to the use of bleach as a source to clean hypodermic needles to combat the spread of disease via intravenous drug use. Ultimately, the band settled on *Bleach* as the album's title. The cover depicted a photograph taken by Tracy Marander on April 1, 1989, at Olympia's Reko Muse art gallery which featured all members of the band, including guitarist Jason Everman. A negative version of the photograph graced the cover of *Bleach* and displayed the band in full aggression. Pavitt had other ideas for the cover, however the band members advocated for Marander's photo. The back cover of the album, printed all in black with white lettering, featured the track list and a summary of the band's personnel: Kurdt Kobain: vocals, guitar; Chris Novoselic: bass; Chad Channing: drums; Jason Everman: guitar. Everman did not perform on the album, however he paid Reciprocal Recording for the recording costs which totaled $606.17.

Everman, a veteran of several local bands, had become familiar with Nirvana in 1988 after his friend Chad Channing had joined the band. The pair resided on Bainbridge Island and had known each other since the fifth grade. Additionally, approximately four years prior, the pair had been in a speed metal band called Stone Crow. At seventeen, Everman began working as a commercial fisherman which paid handsomely and allowed him to save thousands of dollars. Reportedly without any expectations, Everman volunteered to finance Nirvana's recording sessions at Reciprocal Recording. In exchange for Everman's generosity, Cobain eventually chose to credit him on *Bleach*. In February 1989, when the prospect of a second guitarist seemed beneficial to support Cobain during future tours, Everman officially joined Nirvana.

On February 10, 1989, just one month after playing their first show ever outside the boundaries of Washington State, Nirvana embarked on a two week tour of the West Coast which included shows supporting the Melvins and Mudhoney. With months to spare before the release of their debut, the road offered the band alleviation from their frustrations with Sub Pop, along with some needed income. The trek began in San Francisco and featured many new songs which would be included on *Bleach*. Despite the extent of their travels, the band's payment was so bad at San Francisco's Covered Wagon Saloon that they had no money for food and were reportedly forced to eat at a soup kitchen operated by the local Hare Krishnas. Following their second show in San Jose, the brief outing was cut short when Cobain and his girlfriend had to return to Seattle due to illness.

In an attempt to promote Sub Pop, and deter its financial ruination, Pavitt and Poneman paid for the *Melody Maker's* Everett True to be flown from England to Seattle to complete a story about the burgeoning scene. In the March 18, 1989, edition, the *Melody Maker* dedicated a portion of its cover and a lengthy article to Sub Pop and the Seattle music scene. The article, titled "Seattle: Rock City," summarized many of the local bands, including a brief acknowledgement to Nirvana. "Basically, this is the real thing. No rock star contrivance, no intellectual perspective, no master plan for world domination," the article declared. "You're talking about four guys in their twenties from rural Washington who wanna rock, who if they weren't doing this, they would be working in a supermarket or lumber yard, or fixing cars. Kurdt Kobain is also a great tunesmith, although still a relatively young songwriter. He wields a riff with passion." The article was a success and created legions of fans in the United Kingdom for Sub Pops' artists, including Nirvana.

On June 9, 1989, Nirvana played their biggest show to date; Sub Pop's inaugural "Lame Fest," at Seattle's Moore Theatre. As Seattle's oldest theater, which held 1,500 at capacity, the Moore Theatre opened in 1907 and would eventually welcome many international musicians and theatrical productions, but on Friday, June 9, the locals ruled. Advertised in *The Rocket* as "a one night orgy of sweat and insanity," Nirvana opened the all ages show and was followed by TAD and Mudhoney. Nirvana's set allowed the band to feature their new material and, although *Bleach* was not scheduled to be released for six days, copies were sold early at "Lame Fest." Approaching their positions as the show began, instead of the cramped confines of a bar or club stage, the band members found themselves in the uncommon position of being spread out across the largest stage they had ever played. Their set concluded with "Blew" as Novoselic threw his bass into the air and Cobain recklessly swung his guitar over his head by the strap before diving into the drum kit. Rising from the wreckage, Cobain then began to wave goodbye to the audience as his guitar hung from his hair by the strings after becoming tangled during the chaos. Despite minor sound problems during the set, the audience was left amazed and it was evident that Nirvana's live presentation had quickly improved during their short career.

According to a review of the show, published in *Backlash*, Nirvana's performance was "totally intense" and "quite riveting." The show was viewed as a success and as

Pavitt later noted, "That show ignited the city's youth and put Seattle on the map."

On June 15, 1989, *Bleach* was released in the United States to minimal fanfare. The Fine Young Cannibals' *The Ray and the Cooked* was the top album in the country while the New Kids on the Block's "I'll Be Loving You (Forever)" was the top single. Hair metal bands were packing arenas. Teen heartthrobs graced magazine covers.

The first 1,000 copies of *Bleach* were printed on white vinyl, while the second 2,000 copies included a limited edition poster. Sub Pop's catalogue summary described the album as "Hypnotic and righteous heaviness from these Olympia pop stars. They're young, they own their own van, and they're going to make us rich." Although Sub Pop believed *Bleach* was a good album, the label did not promote it like other releases and it was not expected to sell more than 5,000 copies. Despite the lukewarm push, selected tracks from the album began receiving steady airplay on college radio and sales eventually totaled 40,000 copies prior to the release of the band's second album in 1991. Eventually, *Bleach* would go on to sell nearly two million copies in the United States, establishing it as the most successful album in the history of Sub Pop.

Channing later recalled that some of his happiest memories as Nirvana's drummer occurred during the making of *Bleach*. "It's because it was fresh to all of us. We were really excited about it. We thought it was so cool when it came out on vinyl. Or even when the single first came out, we were very up, very amped and optimistic. Everything was going the way we wanted it to - it was cool. I think those were the best times - may have been for them too, I don't know."

The album also began to receive critical acclaim from several publications. According to the July 8, 1989, edition of the *New Musical Express*, "This is the biggest, baddest sound that Sub Pop have so far managed to unearth. So primitive that they manage to make label mates Mudhoney sound like Genesis, Nirvana turn up the volume and spit and claw their way to the top of the musical garbage heap." An article by Everett True, published in an October 1989 edition of the *Melody Maker*, further lauded Nirvana and their first album: "Where Nirvana differs from most of their contemporaries is in the strength of Kurdt's songwriting. Among those in the know, Nirvana are said to be the cream of the crop (if they can get their live show together). Listen to the wickedly named *Bleach* Sub Pop LP and you can hear those roots showing—far from being a melting potpourri of every loud noise imaginable, Nirvana crafts their songs with a diligence not seen this side of Creation. "Blew," "About a Girl," "Big Cheese" (the first mind-fuck of a single), "Sifting"; all these songs are crafted round a firm base of tune, chorus, harmony."

6

FULL CIRCLE

As Nirvana gained attention, largely due to the release of *Bleach* and the power of their live shows, Sub Pop hoped to capitalize. On June 21, 1989, with plans to take just over one month, Nirvana began a twenty-six date U.S. club tour in Seattle in support of *Bleach*. Following a show at the Vogue, Nirvana left the Emerald City early the next morning in Novoselic's newly acquired secondhand white Dodge van. Aptly nicknamed "The Van," the vehicle would ultimately carry the band across thousands of miles and through three U.S. tours while never breaking down. With no formal management acquired for the band by Sub Pop, Novoselic addressed many of the responsibilities himself, including their schedule and finances, while utilizing "The Van" as an office. Exhibiting patterns of micromanagement during the band's journey, Novoselic monitored the vehicle's speed and the use of the air conditioning to ensure money was not spent frivolously. In addition to the band and their instruments, personal necessities and merchandise filled the vehicle, including the band's now famous T-shirt which featured the band's name, an illustration of Dante's Circles of Hell, and the phrase "Nirvana: Fudge Packin', Crack Smokin', Satan Worshippin' Motherfuckers." The slogan had been randomly scribbled on a wall in jest by Novoselic and, after Cobain took notice, it was incorporated on a T-shirt that was being designed by the lead singer which, like the *Bleach* sessions, was financed by Everman. The T-shirt sold well, but at some shows police officers felt it was offensive and directed attendees seen wearing it to turn it inside out.

On June 22, after a thirteen hour trek across 800 miles and less than twenty-four hours after their show at the Vogue, Nirvana performed at San Francisco's Covered Wagon Saloon before continuing south to bars and clubs in Los Angeles, Long Beach, Tempe, and Santa Fe. The band's stop in Los Angeles included a show at Al's Bar, the oldest punk club on the West Coast, in addition to a performance the same day on a small stage confined to the back of Rhino Records in what was their first ever in-store gig.

The first ten days of the tour saw the band traveling at a blistering pace throughout the West Coast and Midwest. Everyone took turns behind the wheel except Cobain whose apprehensive driving routinely brought the van to an awkward crawl. At each stop, in what was a common position during their initial treks, the band was either opening or performing mid-card. Opening primarily with "School" and closing with "Blew," the band's setlists during the tour included nearly every track from *Bleach*, along with several unreleased tracks. The average setlist included "School," "Floyd the Barber," "Love Buzz," "Dive," "Spank Thru," "Scoff," "Breed," "About a Girl," "Big Cheese," "In Bloom," "Molly's Lips," "Been a Son," "Stain," "Negative Creep," and "Blew."

As the tour progressed, attendance varied from city to city, partially due to the scarcity of *Bleach* in some record stores. While the turnouts in the Midwest and Texas proved to be largely scant, crowds on the East Coast grew with the assistance of heavy college radio airplay. Regardless of the crowd's size, the band's passion and unique stage appearance was not lost on their fans and critics. "They looked so odd," Sonic Youth's Thurston Moore later recalled. "They were like Children of the Corn or something like that. We had no sense about what we were seeing, but each song was amazing."

Having barely been outside the Pacific Northwest prior to the tour, the allure of leaving Seattle and exploring the United States was exciting for the band. In the van, their conversations were typical as they listened to various compilations and albums by the Vaselines, the Beatles, Led Zeppelin, Tallulah Gosh, and Motorhead. Although they lacked consistent rest, food, money, and battled monotony, morale was high within the band during the initial dates of the tour. Despite their enthusiasm, frustration soon set in due to a lack of financial support from Sub Pop. Although local promoters were expected to find a location for the band to sleep at each stop, which was typically the apartment floor of a fan or a fellow musician, several nights they were forced to sleep in their van or camp on the side of the road. On one occasion, following a show in Texas, the weary band slept outside a dense swamp while parked near a sign that warned, "Beware of the Alligators." They ultimately slept with baseball bats and two-by-fours at their sides. Travel throughout the southern states caused the van to become miserably hot. Additionally, because the air conditioning was rationed at the direction of Novoselic, there was little relief. As a result, the heat warped numerous copies of *Bleach* the band intended to sell at tour stops.

Like attendance during their lengthy U.S. tour, payment guarantees were equally as imbalanced. At times the band averaged no more than $100 a night, but payments could be low as $25. On one occasion, following the band's show at Santa Fe's Sun Club, club management failed to pay the band the agreed $50 for their performance. As a result of their inconsistent pay, at times the band was forced to choose between gas or food. When they were able to eat, corn dogs or fast food from 7/11 or McDonald's were common options, while Novoselic, the band's only vegetarian, grazed supermarket salad bars. Though his diet on the road likely did not help his condition, Cobain's undiagnosed stomach ailment continued to cause him discomfort and he began to vomit regularly during the tour. He later described the pain as "the worst stomach flu you can imagine." Additionally, the poor conditions in the van made Cobain susceptible to a number of pulmonary related illnesses which he was prone to catch even in the most stable of environments. At times, because of his poor health and chronic pain, Cobain could be found isolated in the van in the fetal position.

Carrying on in the tradition of Jimi Hendrix and the Who, the band began to destroy their equipment following most shows. It began randomly in 1988 during a Halloween party at Evergreen State College and would continue throughout the remainder of their career. In addition to the destruction of Cobain's guitar, Novoselic would join in as well. At times, Cobain would hurl himself into Channing's drum kit, albeit guaranteeing that an encore would not occur. As a result of the musicians' cathartic release, shrapnel from their instruments was propelled across the stage; a splintered neck, a barreling body, an airborne cymbal, or a falling speaker stack. Novoselic would later describe the destruction as nothing more than a gimmick meant to end any performance in spectacular fashion. "It didn't matter if we played great or if we played horrible; you smash your gear and it's a stellar ending to the set." Because of the destruction, the band would spend the following day searching area pawn shops for a cheap replacement guitar or bass only to repeat the destruction at the next show. On some occasions, if the band lacked expendable funds, Sub Pop would Fed Ex a guitar or Cobain repaired the damaged equipment himself using parts from prior victims. Years later, and sadly no longer a necessity, Novoselic would still instinctually scan pawn shop windows for cheap left handed guitars.

On July 15, at a show in Jamaica Plain, Massachusetts, after damaging his only guitar at the previous show and unable to secure a replacement, Cobain performed a nine song set before the approximate thirty in attendance without a guitar subsequently leaving the guitar responsibilities solely to Everman. By all accounts, Cobain never performed a full show again without a guitar strapped to his back.

"We were totally poor, but God, we were seeing the United States for the first time," Cobain later recounted fondly. "And we were in a band and we were making enough money to survive. It was awesome. It was just great."

Although Cobain had welcomed the presence of an additional guitarist on stage, tension with Everman began almost immediately after the tour commenced. As a band focused solely on the impassioned presentation of their music, Everman's affinity for showmanship was met with exasperation by his bandmates, particularly Cobain. "He was like a peacock on amphetamines," the lead singer later described. "It was embarrassing." Further strain occurred following the aforementioned Massachusetts show on July 15, when Everman invited a woman back to his room following the band's performance. Cobain and Novoselic considered the act misogynistic and in poor taste and, as a result, Everman's position in the band was tarnished further. He also withdrew and became quiet toward his bandmates which made travel awkward within the tight confines of Novoselic's van. Despite Everman's declining status within the band, his eventual departure was a surprise to some, with the exception of Cobain and Novoselic.

Following a show on July 18, 1989, at New York City's Pyramid Club, and prior to the band's plans to continue north for scheduled shows in Canada, the final two weeks of the tour were abruptly canceled at Cobain's insistence. A sly plan to flee while leaving Everman at the apartment of an acquaintance was scrapped and everyone eventually made the 3,000 mile trek home together. The stress of firing Everman hung in the air between Cobain and Novoselic throughout the three day journey, during which few words were spoken and the van stopped for nothing more than food and gas. Following the band's return to Washington, Everman was never formally fired, or repaid for financing *Bleach*, he was just never called again. Cobain and Novoselic historically struggled with confrontation, largely to avoid hurt feelings, an issue they had grappled with when their former drummers were passively dismissed. In December 1989, Cobain informed *The Rocket* that Everman's dismissal was a "very mutual decision" due to "artistic differences." His relatively neutral position would later change when he claimed that Everman was not repaid as a result of "mental damages" incurred. Contrary to Cobain's recollection at the time, Everman would later claim that he had quit the band. "I came to the realization that my role in the band was essentially going to be the rhythm-guitar player," he described. "I had the desire and inclination to write, as well." Overall, Everman's only studio session with Nirvana occurred in the spring of 1989 at Evergreen State College. During the session, the band covered Kiss' "Do You Love Me" which was later included on the 1990 release *Hard to Believe: A Kiss Covers Compilation*.

In the Fall of 1989, Everman joined Soundgarden after their bass player, Hiro Yamamoto, suddenly quit the band to return to college. Struggling to find his place in Soundgarden, Everman's tenure with the band was short-lived and he was fired in mid-1990 following the completion of the band's *Louder Than Love* tour. Soon after, Everman relocated to New York where he secured employment, however in 1994, after having been influenced by the Renaissance icon Benvenuto Cellini, Everman enlisted in the United States Army. He subsequently served in the Army's 2nd Ranger Battalion and later in the Special Forces. Following the terrorist attacks on September 11, 2001, Everman was deployed to Afghanistan and later Iraq. When his military service ended, Everman earned a Bachelor of Arts degree in philosophy from Columbia University School of General Studies and later pursued sailing as a past time resulting in thousands of logged nautical miles. Everman's life truly became the stuff of legend. In 2013, while recounting his experiences during an interview with *The New York Times*, Everman recalled his departure from Nirvana: "To be honest, I never really had any expectations about the gig. It just ended."

Now in a brief holding pattern after the *Bleach* tour ended prematurely, Cobain and Novoselic developed a side project with the Screaming Trees' Mark Lanegan and Mark Pickerel. For months, Cobain and Lanegan had been writing songs and both were developing an appreciation for the blues. The band dubbed themselves The Jury and quickly entered Reciprocal Recording on August 20 and 28, focusing on cover versions of tracks originally written and recorded by Huddie "Lead Belly" Ledbetter. A folk and blues singer residing in the southern United States during the early decades of the 20th century, Lead Belly was proficient on the twelve-string guitar and wrote songs focusing on racism, prison, and women. He was later credited by Bob Dylan for his own introduction to folk. An acquaintance introduced Cobain to Lead Belly the previous year, but his interest was heightened further after reading an article by William S. Burroughs in which Lead Belly's music was described as "something with real soul." Cobain devoured Lead Belly's albums and felt a connection with his music more so than any artist he had ever experienced. "I'd hope that my songs approximate that honesty. That's what I strive for," he explained to Everett True in 1992. The prospect of covering the deceased bluesman captivated him.

Produced by Jack Endino, The Jury's sessions resulted in recordings of "They Hung Him On a Cross," "Grey Goose," "Where Did You Sleep Last Night," and "Ain't It a Shame." Cobain's rendition of the latter would later be hailed as one of the greatest vocal performances of his career, while Nirvana's own eventual cover of "Where Did You Sleep Last Night" was critically acclaimed. Although the band had hoped to complete an album, The Jury would never convene again. Lanegan later attributed the poor output to the lead singers' hesitation to not disrespect the other by assuming a leadership role. The Jury's cover of "Where Did You Sleep Last Night" was released in 1990 as part of Lanegan's solo album, *The Winding Sheet*, however the remaining tracks would not receive an official release for fifteen years.

The studio was a common place in August 1989 and, once again a three piece, Nirvana entered Seattle's Music Source studio with producer Steve Fisk to record tracks for an upcoming EP titled *Blew*. The resulting EP featured two previously released tracks, "Blew" and "Love Buzz," in addition to "Been a Son" and "Stain," both of which were recorded with Fisk. "Even In His Youth," "Token Eastern Song," and an unfinished version of "Polly" were also recorded during the session. Like *Bleach*, the cover featured a photograph by Tracy Marander. The band's original plan was to release the EP as a promotional tool for a forthcoming European tour, however it was delayed. Eventually, 3,000 copies of the *Blew* EP were released in November 1989, by Tupelo Records exclusively in the United Kingdom. The EP peaked at number one on the Independent charts within one month.

With an obligation to complete the cancelled dates from two months prior, Nirvana embarked on a brief tour of the Midwest in late September 1989. Now leaving Washington with a U-Haul rental trailer carrying their equipment, the additional space in the van allowed for passengers. Ben Shepherd joined the trek as a roadie and quickly acclimated well to the band and the close confines of their travels. A resident of Bainbridge Island, Shepherd was a friend and former bandmate of Channing's and a competent musician in his own right. As a result, Cobain briefly considered the possibility of offering Shepherd the second guitarist position left vacant after the dismissal of Everman. After several friends advised him against adding a second guitarist, Cobain concurred and felt that the band's sound as a trio worked best. Interestingly, less than one year later, Shepherd would join Soundgarden as their bass player following Everman's termination. Along with Shepherd, a sound man also joined the tour. Shortly following the release of *Bleach*, Jonathan Poneman introduced the band to engineer Craig Montgomery with the hope that he could provide assistance on the road. Montgomery had worked with several Seattle bands and had heard rumblings about Nirvana and the intensity of Cobain. "I saw my job as connecting Kurt's voice to the audience," he described years later. Montgomery remained a fixture with the band and worked every Nirvana show during the subsequent four years.

After a stop at Seattle's the Vogue on September 26, the band traveled 1,700 miles to Minneapolis' Uptown Bar followed by Chicago's Cabaret Metro. Overall, attendance fluctuated during the brief trek, including 200 in Chicago and less than two dozen in Boulder on October 13, however payment guarantees for the band had risen to between $100 to $200 per night. It was slowly becoming clear with each passing show, regardless of the crowd size, that the band's fanbase was growing. In Omaha on October 8, the crowd's cheers led to a rare encore from the band that included a brief segue into "Where Did You Last Sleep Last Night" and an early version of "Breed."

Largely tension free without the presence of Everman, the band's return to the road was still dealt with stress. Cobain's stomach ailment persisted and after collapsing in Minneapolis he was brought to the emergency room by Novoselic. Despite his frail appearance and obvious discomfort, doctors were left perplexed by his condition. Cobain later estimated that during the next four years he consulted fifteen different doctors and was prescribed fifty different types of medication, but the condition persisted. Many attributed Cobain's struggle to a poor diet, but he was ignorant to the conjecture and continued to live off of nutritionally rewarding sustenance such as hot dogs and macaroni and cheese. Compounded by Cobain's condition, Novoselic had developed an increasing pattern of alcohol abuse. Alcohol had become part of his performance regimen, so much so that each host venue during the U.S. tour agreed to provide a case of beer. As a result, Novoselic spent a majority of the band's shows intoxicated. His inebriation would lead to ranting, typically about the concept of love, followed by various antics until he would eventually pass out hours later. In 1992, Cobain explained the extent of Novoselic's imbibing. "When he drinks, he drinks to the point of oblivion - he turns into literally a retard. He can't speak. All he can do is gesture and knock things over."

On October 13, the United States portion of the tour concluded. Following expenses, the band returned to Washington with roughly $300 each, but the modest sum quantified to success. The band members briefly separated and settled for rest before departing one week later on their first overseas tour.

In late October, Nirvana departed from Sea-Tac Airport on a forty-two day, thirty-six date, European tour of nine nations, titled "Heavier Than Heaven." During the trek, the band was joined by label mates TAD and the two bands rotated the headlining spot at each appearance. In August, two months after its June release in the United States, *Bleach* was released to stellar reviews in Europe. In an attempt to promote the band further prior to the tour, a Sub Pop publicist submitted an artist bio to overseas media. The somewhat comedic release noted that the band was now a three piece and described Cobain as "perfecting the garage attendant style," Novoselic as a competitive tree climber, and Channing as appearing "perpetually stoned."

On October 23, in what was Nirvana's first show outside of North America, the band performed at the Riverside, located in Newcastle, England. Like the U.S. tour, the European tour saw Nirvana opening primarily with "School" and closing with "Blew." The average setlist included "School," "Scoff," "Love Buzz," "Floyd the Barber," "Dive," "Polly," "Big Cheese," "About a Girl," "Spank Thru,"

"Mr. Moustache," "Breed," "Been a Son," "Negative Creep,"
"Stain" and "Blew."

Every opportunity was utilized by Nirvana during the
trek to promote the tour along with their burgeoning career.
On October 26, during a night off following shows in
Manchester and Leeds, the band entered Maida Vale Studios
in London to record four tracks for the "John Peel Show." By
1989, disc jockey John Peel had become an institution on
England's BBC Radio 1 and an early advocate of legendary
British acts Led Zeppelin, David Bowie, and Pink Floyd.
Beginning in 1967, Peel's show had become known for
promoting and introducing the country to countless acts on
the "Peel Sessions." During their own session, Nirvana
opened with what was at that time their best known track
"Love Buzz," followed by "About a Girl," and "Polly," before
closing with "Spank Thru." The session was produced by
Dale Griffin who later noted how well rehearsed the band
was, as opposed to most bands that appeared on the show.
The performance was broadcast the following month, on
November 22, 1989, and was later heavily bootlegged as
Nirvana's popularity grew. Peel's support helped the band
secure a growing fanbase in England which led to additional
"Peel Sessions" in 1990 and 1991.

In the November 4 issue of the *Melody Maker*, the
"Heavier Than Heaven" tour was reviewed following an
October 27 stop at London's School of Oriental and African
Studies. "Kurdt Cobain - his skinny frame lost in the space
vacated by TAD - has a voice to reduce grown men to tears,
and the sort of hoarse, anguished cry that can turn a good
song into an unforgettable one. And this band have plenty of

those, no problem. Nirvana work from their own rock blueprint, pushing their songs through an emotional and physical grinder, each one edging towards a private precipice inside Cobain's mind." The review lauded the band and concluded by noting, "You can't argue or reason with stuff like this. Nirvana are superb, cranked-up, desperate and fucking loud."

On Halloween, the band left the United Kingdom by ferry for several shows in the Netherlands. Sound issues plagued the band during many of their stops before moving on to West Germany, however their final show at Amsterdam's Melkweg proved to be one of the tour's highlights. The powerful eighteen song setlist, which included a jam, a smashed guitar, and a two song encore, was met by a stunned audience.

During the tour, eleven men, which included members of Nirvana, TAD, and the latter's 300-plus- pound lead singer Tad Doyle, drove from city to city in a Fiat van, which was designed to comfortably sit six to nine passengers. At times, between shows, the rigid schedule required overnight travel while passengers slept upright within the close confines of the van which also carried the bands' equipment and merchandise. When time allowed, random bed and breakfasts were acquired for the outfit. Upon arrival, and as the weary passengers staggered out of the Fiat van to their rooms, those present at the typical family run establishments were left alarmed by the unique sight.

Despite the difficulties, the tour received largely stellar reviews and nearly every show was sold out. This was contrary to the American tour, whereas numerous venues in America were at most half full, and a clear signal that Europe was the first domino to fall for Nirvana. "People seemed to know who we were," Novoselic later recalled. "And it seemed to us that we were more popular there than we were at home."

On November 11, two days after the Berlin Wall fell, Nirvana entered Germany's capital city to play at the Ecstasy. Novoselic later described a scene of jubilance with cars lined bumper to bumper for sixty miles waiting to exit East Germany. Once inside Berlin the scene resembled a party on a scale similar to that of New York's Time Square during the annual New Year's Eve celebration. Interestingly, although history was being made out in the streets, and somewhat indicative of the response the tour was receiving across Europe, the club was still half-full by show time. The biggest party in the world was happening and Nirvana and TAD were on stage.

Initial excitement and shenanigans in the van quickly changed to stress due to sleep deprivation, hunger, and the dizzying tour schedule across Europe. No one struggled with the dynamics more so than Cobain who quickly became exhausted and homesick. He missed his girlfriend desperately and wrote to her often. One postcard, mailed by Cobain just days following his arrival in Europe, was covered over and over again with the phrase "I love you." As the tour dragged on, Sub Pop's Bruce Pavitt and Jonathan Poneman flew to Rome unannounced to accompany the bands. Although the bosses' motivation to check in on the tour was genuine, many within the bands took issue with the pair flying comfortably while a tight van was their first class. Almost immediately it became clear to Pavitt and Poneman that Cobain needed a break.

On November 27, ten songs into Nirvana's set at the Piper Club in Rome, Cobain suffered what Pavitt later described as "a nervous breakdown on stage." In a moment of clear emotional distress exacerbated by persistent sound issues, Cobain smashed his guitar during "Spank Thru" and proceeded to climb to the top of a tall stack of speakers where he stood for several minutes overlooking the audience. As the stack swayed side to side, Cobain threatened to jump as intoxicated members of the audience heartlessly chanted "Jump!" With assistance from the club's security, Cobain eventually came down and managed to complete the set, but he remained distressed and burst into tears backstage following the show. He proceeded to walk outside with Poneman where he began to rant, demanded to go home to his girlfriend, and exclaimed he never wanted to play music again. By the end of the night the stress had caused each member of Nirvana to consider quitting the band, but everyone ultimately reconsidered.

The next day, while the band members and the crew drove on to Switzerland in the Fiat van, Poneman, Pavitt, and TAD drummer Steve Wied stayed behind in Rome in an attempt to calm Cobain. While primarily discussing music, the group spent the sunny day walking throughout the city and touring the Coliseum, Saint Peter's Basilica, and the Sistine Chapel. Pavitt and Cobain analyzed their favorite records and discovered that they had both attended the same Black Flag show in 1984. Pavitt later recalled, "Although generally quiet, he would come alive when discussing music. The Pixies, Beat Happening, the Vaselines, Black Flag. We really connected that day as indie-music geeks."

Late in the day, the group boarded a train which carried them throughout the night to the Swiss border. Soon after the train's departure, Cobain placed his wallet and his passport in his shoes as he relaxed and fell asleep. He awoke some time later and discovered that his wallet and his passport had been stolen. Stepping in to assist an emotionally weary Cobain, Pavitt and Poneman worked with Swiss authorities in order to acquire a temporary visa for the Nirvana frontman. After several hours, with the van and the remaining musicians and crew members waiting nearby, Cobain was allowed to enter the country for shows the following days in Geneva and Zurich.

The final show of the "Heavier Than Heaven" tour found Nirvana at London's Astoria Theatre on December 3 for "Lame Fest UK '89." Originally operating as a warehouse in the 1920s, the space was converted to a music venue in 1976 before being demolished in 2009 as part of a redevelopment project. During its thirty plus years of existence, the theatre hosted hundreds of international musicians and bands, including the Washington based acts on that cold December night. Performed in front of a sell out crowd of 2,000 fans and members of the British press, the show featured Mudhoney, Nirvana, and TAD. Mudhoney had arrived in Europe on November 22 for their own tour, but made it a point to join the bill for the special event. Prior to the show, a simple coin toss determined that Nirvana would open, followed by TAD and Mudhoney.

With no time for a proper soundcheck after arriving to the venue late following a long trek from Dover in freezing conditions, Nirvana took the stage and warmed up quickly. Moments later, before the band launched into "School," Cobain exclaimed, "Hello, we're one of the three official representatives of the Seattle Sub Pop scene from Washington State!" Although the band's set had some initial technical difficulties, there was no evidence of decline from over a month on the road. Nirvana's approximate fifty minute set, which included scores of stage divers and ended with the destruction of their equipment, proved to be a success and solidified their continued rise to stardom. TAD and Mudhoney had solid sets, but "Nirvana was the epiphany of the evening," according to Sub Pop's Pavitt. Reviews of the band's performance printed in *Sounds* and *Melody Maker* were stellar and on December 16, 1989, following the conclusion of the European tour, the *New Musical Express* declared, "Nirvana are Sub Pop's answer to the Beatles, pop masters with a sense of hard rock and songs that penetrate the memory of their audience."

7

TRANSITIONS

Following the conclusion of the "Heavier Than Heaven" tour, Krist Novoselic and Shelli Dilley traveled to Yogoslavia to visit Novoselic's father where he had settled several years prior after he and Marija Novoselic were divorced. During the visit, Novoselic and Dilley were engaged. The decision marked the next step in their five year relationship and on December 30, 1989, after returning to Washington, the couple were married in their Tacoma apartment. The simple ceremony was officiated by an acquaintance of Dilley's, while Matt Lukin served as Novoselic's best man. The small apartment was filled with guests, including Cobain, Tracy Marander, Novoselic's mother and members of TAD and Mudhoney. The union became part of a transitional period for the band and those within their orbit; the calm before the storm.

As a new decade began, Cobain continued to write at a rapid pace while Nirvana's position as indie darlings had become set in stone. Culminating with the completion of the "Heavier Than Heaven" tour, the band graced their first full magazine cover in the December 1989 edition of *The Rocket*. Depicting an image captured of the band performing live and featuring a disheveled Novoselic in the foreground amongst an adoring European crowd, the cover assisted with morale impacted by the ups and downs of the tour.

In early January, after two days at Reciprocal Recording with Jack Endino, which focused unsuccessfully on the recording of "Sappy," the band began several shows in and around Seattle followed by a brief tour of the West Coast in February. An increase in their stock, many of Novoselic's former responsibilities were alleviated prior to the New Year with the addition of tour manager, Alex Macleod. Additionally, each show began to slowly provide the band with enough compensation for food AND gas.

Accompanied by TAD, Nirvana proceeded south along the coast toward shows in San Jose, Sacramento, Los Angeles, and San Francisco. For the first time during the band's career, Cobain requested that Nirvana headline. TAD accepted their position as the tour opener, despite their lead singer's reservations.

Hurtling forward into the spring full bore with new material and consistently impactful live shows, the band soon learned that Sub Pop sought to release a new album later in the year. On April 1, 1990, following a show in Chicago, the band travelled throughout the night to Smart Studios, located in Madison, Wisconsin. Smart Studios, which opened in 1983, became the birthplace of many alternative albums in the new decade by bands such as the Smashing Pumpkins, L7, Garbage, and Everclear. With its brick exterior, not far from the state capital, the ordinary building looked like nothing more than an old factory or a warehouse.

At the suggestion of Sub Pop, Nirvana's sessions were booked from April 2 through April 6 with producer Butch Vig, the cofounder of Smart Studios. Following their arrival in Madison, the band checked into the Aloha Inn, a one-star hotel, at a rate of $30 per night. The hotel was considered high end given the band's minimal budget and typical accommodations during prior tours, but the manageable rate allowed them to stay in a comfortable setting throughout the duration of the sessions.

Despite Jonathan Poneman's endorsement of the band, Vig was not overly impressed with *Bleach*, with the exception of "About a Girl." However, as the Smart Studios sessions began, Vig was immediately cognizant of the band's progression, particularly Cobain's songwriting. The sessions were designed to prepare for a second album or an EP, with a release date planned for September 1990, however unlike the *Bleach* sessions the songs presented by the band at Smart Studios were not as developed. Nonetheless, the band's presentation remained solid, with a request for Vig to make them "sound heavy, very heavy," but Cobain's moodiness and propensity to isolate became evident to the producer. "He had these extreme bipolar mood swings," Vig recounted years later. Due to Cobain's emotional separation at times, Vig went to Novoselic to discuss issues. Novoselic, always protective and empathetic toward any perceived criticism of his friend, informed Vig, "he always snaps out of it."

Though the songs presented by the band at Smart Studios were strong, there was not enough time or material to complete a full album. Additionally, Cobain blew his voice out four days into the sessions which impacted the output further. Overall eight songs were recorded, including both old and new compositions: "Dive," "Immodium" (later retitled as "Breed)," "In Bloom," "Sappy" (also known as "Verse Chorus Verse"), "Pay To Play" (also known as "Stay Away)," "Lithium," "Polly," and a cover of the Velvet Underground's "Here She Comes Now." A remixed version of "Polly," recorded during the sessions, would eventually appear on the band's second studio album. Despite the success of the Smart Studios sessions, and initial plans to return by the summer, an inevitable personnel change ultimately delayed the completion of an album.

Once the Smart Studios sessions concluded, the band immediately transitioned back to a brief tour throughout the Midwest, East Coast, and Canada. In late April, between shows in New York and New Jersey, the band filmed a music video for "In Bloom." The video featured footage of the band randomly walking throughout lower Manhattan, in addition to footage from their performance April 28 at Maxwell's located in Hoboken, New Jersey. Appearing bald in some scenes, Novoselic had shaved his head in an act of expiation for what he believed was a poor performance on April 26 at the Pyramid Club in Manhattan.

Audience attendance at each tour stop remained strong and the band's fan base was growing, however Cobain's frustration with Channing's drumming had become increasingly evident. His timing had become an issue and Cobain had always hoped for a drummer that hit hard. During the Smart Studios sessions, despite Butch Vig's support of Channing due to his own experience behind the kit, Cobain's criticism of his drummer had been routine. The lead singer knew the sound he wanted the band to attain and expected his drummer to oblige. "Chad would be playing something and Kurt would go, 'Stop, stop, stop, let me show you' then get on the drums and show him the fills that he wanted," Vig recalled years later. Channing's kit subsequently became a routine target for his bandmates' frustrations during shows late in the tour. "I got so pissed off at Chad that I'd jump into the drum set, then smash my guitar," Cobain later described to Michael Azzerad. Duct tape became a necessity for Channing to keep the drums operational until the spring trek concluded in mid-May. Research sources provide conflicting dates, however the tour's last show would prove to be Channing's final performance with Nirvana.

Despite the moderate success of the Smart Studios sessions and interest that was beginning to generate from major labels, Cobain and Novoselic chose to fire Channing after the band returned to Washington. In late May, the pair traveled to Channing's home on Bainbridge Island, a thirty minute ferry ride from Seattle, in order to deliver the news. Neither Cobain or Novoselic had dismissed their prior drummers in such a courteous manner, so the act of meeting with Channing was indicative of how they felt about him as a person. The multi-instrumentalist took his dismissal calmly, largely because his hopes of being a contributing songwriter within the band were not being met. Cobain and Novoselic exchanged hugs with Channing and the pair left. Cobain later acknowledged, "I felt like I'd just killed somebody." As time passed Channing was never heard disparaging his former bandmates and years later, during an interview with KAOS TV, Channing recalled his old band with fondness. "I have no regrets because I always thought that things just sort of fall in place for a reason. For example, I was that perfect puzzle piece for the band at the time, and then they needed another piece to do other things and stuff. Our differences were strictly on a musical level. We always stayed friends."

Contrary to the band's presumed dreariness, they always maintained a mischievous spirit. Beginning with the addition of Channing, the band's time spent together off stage was typically lighthearted and quirky. As years have passed, Channing has recounted various tales, including a story of his time behind the wheel of the band's touring van. During one long trek through Montana, and as his bandmates slept, Channing passed the time driving with his teeth. Novoselic eventually awoke with a shriek at the sight in the driver's seat. "That's one of the things that made Nirvana so great," Sub Pop's Poneman later described. "There was this whimsical, childlike, silly thing that they had going on. They managed to have that and still be incredibly cool; it wasn't like this fey, contrived thing. It was who they were that informed what they were and how they projected themselves, but they were total rock star studs at the same time."

During the years following his dismissal from Nirvana, Channing married and started a family. Additionally, he continued to seek new musical endeavors and formed three bands during the next twenty years; Fire Ants, The Methodists, and Before Cars. Channing's contributions to Nirvana were never questioned and remained evident during the band's remaining years, including the drum grooves he had written for some songs which were eventually used by his replacement and incorporated onto the band's second album.

In addition to personnel changes, Cobain chose to make changes within his personal life. A distance had grown between he and Tracy Marander during the early months of 1990 and culminated when Cobain slept with another woman during Nirvana's brief spring tour. Cobain had never been unfaithful before and his actions were simply indicative of where his relationship with Marander stood. On April 27, he contacted Marander from Massachusetts and suggested that the pair should separate. Although they continued to live together for a short period following Cobain's return from the tour, until Marander could save enough money for an apartment closer to work, their relationship had come to an end. "I think he pretty much didn't love me as much as he used to or felt," Marander rationalized years later. "He just felt like maybe he was moving ahead and I wasn't." Eventually, in July, Marander moved out of the Olympia apartment she and Cobain had shared for nearly three years. Cobain did not have consistent employment, however the small profits he had earned from touring allowed him to stay in the apartment.

Once Marander's irritation toward Cobain subsided, the former couple spoke often and she continued to champion his musical endeavors. "He was a really good artist. It gets lost sometimes that he was a good artist. It also gets lost that he smiled a lot" and "he was a nice guy and wanted to think the best of people," Marander recalled in Greg Prato's *Grunge Is Dead*.

Soon after he and Marander had separated, Cobain began dating Tobi Vail, a musician and member of the band

Bikini Kill, who he had met years prior when he was a member of the "Cling Ons." A resident of Olympia, Vail had become friends with Cobain in the spring of 1988, along with Marander. After his separation, Cobain's feelings for Vail developed quickly. His affection became so intense that, during the first full evening the pair spent together, the excitement caused him to become physically sick. His lyrics in "Aneurysm" would later summarize the event.

The conditions within Cobain's apartment changed dramatically without Marander's presence. Dishes piled up, the animals were largely unkempt, and the resulting smell permeated the air. Contrary to Marander's motherly efforts and the support she provided Cobain, Vail was a feminist and not interested in a traditional relationship or kowtowing to a man's needs.

As 1990 moved on, and Nirvana was no closer to the release of an EP or LP, Sub Pop hoped to release a new single. Additionally, with the band's increasing popularity, Sub Pop was becoming uncertain about their own ability to contend with offers from major labels. Although the Smart Studios sessions were meant to culminate in the band's second album, bootlegs of the sessions quickly served as demos for major labels. As regional standouts Mother Love Bone, Soundgarden, and Alice In Chains had already done, Nirvana's transition was inevitable.

With Dan Peters of Mudhoney on drums, on July 11, 1990, Nirvana entered Reciprocal Recording to record the basics for what would be their new single, "Sliver." The single was largely written over the course of several days in rehearsals and recorded during an approximate one hour session using TAD's equipment while Tad Doyle and his bandmates were on a dinner break. TAD graciously allowed for the intrusion during their own session after Jonathan Poneman contacted Jack Endino, who was recording TAD, and begged for the studio time. Two weeks later, Cobain returned to Reciprocal Recording and recorded his vocals for the song. "Dive," which had been recorded by Butch Vig during the Smart Studios sessions, was chosen as the single's B-side. The "Sliver" / "Dive" single was released in September and both tracks from the single were eventually included on the band's 1992 compilation, *Incesticide*.

Without the availability of Peters due to Mudhoney's commitment to a European festival tour, Nirvana was forced to look elsewhere for a drummer during a proposed August tour with Sonic Youth; a New York based quartet that Cobain and Novoselic revered. Following the conclusion of Mudhoney's tour in September, Peters planned to return to Nirvana for rehearsals and some live performances. In the interim, Dale Crover of the Melvins subsequently agreed to fill in during Nirvana's brief tour with only one simple condition: "Do not jump into my drum set!"

Prior to the start of the brief tour, Cobain and Novoselic drove to San Francisco, along with sound technician Craig Montgomery, to pick up Crover. On August 10, before the van departed from the city, Buzz Osborne insisted that everyone should go to see Scream that night; a Washington, D.C. based hardcore punk band playing at the

Chatterbox. Following the show, Cobain noted to others that he wished Nirvana could secure a full time drummer who hit as hard as Scream's drummer. At the time, a twenty-one-year-old sat behind Scream's drum kit named Dave Grohl.

Raised in Virginia, Dave Grohl developed an interest in music at a young age. He was encouraged by his parents who were both active in music at times in their lives; his father a flutist and his mother a singer. Like Cobain and Novoselic, an interest in 70s rock during his early teens led Grohl to other genres, including new wave and punk. He became obsessed with Led Zeppelin and worshipped John Bonham. Grohl set his sights on the drums, obsessively teaching himself to play in his bedroom using a makeshift kit built out of pillows, chairs, and his bed. He played along with Bonham, in addition to Rush's Neil Peart and Slayer's Dave Lombardo, at times to the point of exhaustion. "I would play to these records until there was condensation dripping from the windows," he explained to *Modern Drummer* in 2004. Although he also played guitar, Grohl's drumming intensity was prodigious. His playing became a sight to behold; as if he were created in a lab from the DNA of Bonham and the Who's Keith Moon. He jammed with neighborhood friends and joined several bands during his teens while he waited for a transition which was all but assured.

Randomly in 1986, Grohl walked into a music store and discovered an advertisement stating "Scream: Looking for drummer." Scream had become legends of the Washington, D.C. hardcore scene and the possibility of joining the band intrigued Grohl. He contacted Franz Stahl, the band's guitarist, quit high school soon after, and, after lying to Stahl about his age, Grohl eventually joined Scream. His addition was seamless and, despite his young age, Grohl's savage style quickly earned him a reputation as one of the hardest hitting drummers in the music industry.

Touring was constant for nearly four years, however in 1990, after the band's bassist unexpectedly departed due to drug problems, Scream disbanded. Barely twenty-one, Grohl settled in Los Angeles and acquired work tiling floors. Uncertain about his future, Grohl eventually spoke to Buzz Osborne, whom he had met when the Melvins and Scream crossed paths while touring in Europe. Aware of Nirvana's continuous struggle to maintain the services of a full time drummer, Osborne thought Grohl's style would be a perfect fit for the band. Ever the band's quasi guardian angel, Osborne provided Grohl with Novoselic's phone number. Soon after, Grohl coordinated a meeting with Cobain and Novoselic and, on September 21, he packed his equipment, along with a bag of clothes, and flew to Seattle.

As the Friday afternoon commuter traffic began to grow, Cobain and Novoselic waited patiently in Novoselic's van outside the Sea-Tac Airport terminal for Grohl's arrival. With little else known other the Virginian's ferocious drumming, Cobain and Novoselic hoped for a harmonious outcome. Their struggle to secure the perfect drummer continued, along with the risk of becoming a punchline among their peers. Shortly after his plane's arrival, Grohl promptly exited the terminal and climbed into the van with a smile toward Cobain and Novoselic. He later described that at first glance the pair "looked like dirty fucking biker children" as he took his seat near Cobain. As Novoselic pulled the van away from the curb for the approximate thirty minute drive to Tacoma, and in attempt to ease any mutual anxiety, Grohl turned to Cobain and offered him an apple. Cobain looked down toward the apple with a wince and stated, "No thanks. It'll make my teeth bleed." The trio were quiet throughout the remainder of the trip as a wide-eyed awkwardness filled the van.

With nearly 1,500 in attendance, Peters played his only show as Nirvana's drummer on September 22 at Seattle's Motor Sports International and Garage. Although their one time mentors the Melvins were on the bill, Nirvana took the stage last in what was their biggest headlining gig to date. The show was a chaotic scene, on a makeshift stage, with a keg of beer strategically placed nearby, and no security anywhere in the building. Audience members consistently jumped on the stage throughout the show in a frenzied manner, knocking over mics, stepping on cords, and leaping from the stage in sheer abandon, resulting in numerous set disruptions. The setlist included the debut of several tracks recorded during the Smart Studios sessions, including "Pay to Play" (also known as "Stay Away") and "Immodium" (later retitled as "Breed"). Somewhat puzzled, Grohl watched the show from the crowd due to the concern and questions some felt his presence would create backstage, particularly Cobain. Several songs into the set, and not overly impressed with the band's performance, Grohl stepped outside and spent the remainder of the set talking with a friend.

Soon after the Motor Sports International Garage show, Cobain and Novoselic scheduled a formal audition with Grohl at the Dutchman, a relatively rundown rehearsal space in Seattle. No more than two minutes into Grohl's thunderous audition, Cobain and Novoselic realized they had found the band's missing piece. With Grohl's exceptional drumming, and further contribution as a background vocalist, his addition to Nirvana was unquestionable. Cobain later recalled the adulation he and Novoselic had for Grohl's abilities and the excitement that was created by adding him to their band. "You can't pass up an opportunity to play with the drummer of our dreams, which is Dave."

On September 25, just hours after Grohl auditioned for Nirvana, Cobain appeared unannounced on KAOS radio's "Boy Meets Girl" show to perform an acoustic set which included "Lithium," "Been a Son," "Polly," "Dumb," and "Opinion." During the set, Cobain proclaimed that he and Novoselic had recruited Nirvana's newest drummer. He stated further, "His name is Dave and he's a baby Dale Crover."

Unfortunately, Nirvana's big news had yet to be revealed to Peters who had assumed he was the band's new drummer. Peters' assumption was reasonable and, according to the drummer, just weeks prior when he questioned his spot in the band, Cobain and Novoselic "were like, 'No, no, no, you're going to be the guy.'" Although he was disappointed when he eventually learned that he had lost his spot in Nirvana, Peters quickly transitioned to playing on a tour with the Screaming Trees before returning to Mudhoney when the band re-formed soon after.

On October 11, with approximately 500 in attendance, Grohl played his first show as Nirvana's drummer at Olympia's North Shore Surf Club, which to his amazement sold out very quickly. Unlike usual shows, the band's set list began with three covers; the Vaselines' "Son of a Gun" and "Molly's Lips," along with the Wipers' "D-7." Unfortunately, the celebratory show was initially plagued by light and sound problems which prompted Novoselic to quip from the stage that someone needed to pay the electricity bill. He followed with, "You can get government aid and stuff if you can't afford it."

Grohl's impact on the band was quickly evident when, early in the show, he hit with such power and ferocity that he broke through the head of his snare drum. Cobain proceeded to lift the snare up in triumph, in full view of the audience, further introducing the world to Nirvana's new drummer. "I felt I had something to prove," Grohl later recalled. "I didn't know anyone - no one in the audience, no one in the band. I was completely on my own. That was the only thing that mattered, that hour on stage. That's what I focused on."

Over a period of four months, Nirvana's new lineup rehearsed most nights for three hours inside a small barn in Tacoma and chemistry was quickly established. Adding to morale, in late October the band traveled to the United Kingdom in support of the "Sliver / Dive" single and played a handful of shows to packed houses averaging a thousand fans a night. Soon after the addition of Grohl, it was quickly evident that a brotherhood had formed within the band and a musical apex would soon be attained. "Nirvana was now a beast that walked the earth," Novoselic described many years later.

Outside of Nirvana, Grohl knew very few in the Northwest and he was largely on his own. After joining the band, Grohl briefly resided with Novoselic and his wife in Tacoma, but with space available in his North Pear Street apartment, Cobain invited him to move in. The dynamic proved successful and, despite Cobain's ongoing struggle with cleanliness and order, the pair grew close. Grohl slept in the living room on a tattered couch covered in cigarette burns and too small to accommodate his six foot frame, however he was kept company by Cobain's pet turtles living in a large tank just feet away. Outside of rehearsals and shows, the housemates passed the time playing Nintendo and shooting at random objects outside the apartment with a BB gun. Lead Belly and Mark Lanegan were on heavy rotation in the apartment, the latter's *The Winding Sheet* becoming one of Grohl's favorite albums over time. "That was the soundtrack to my first six months in Olympia. I listened to it every day—when the sun wouldn't come up, when it went down too early, and when it was cold and raining. I was lonely." Some nights, after Cobain's bedroom light went out and Grohl struggled to fall asleep due to the turtles endlessly banging their heads and shells against the glass tank, he quietly strummed an acoustic guitar. The privacy would serve Grohl well during the infancy of his own eventual transition as a singer and songwriter.

8

"HELLO, WE'RE MAJOR LABEL CORPORATE ROCK SELLOUTS"

Three years prior, while still residing in Aberdeen, Cobain discovered that an acquaintance had begun to experiment with heroin. Although drug use was far from foreign in his own life, indulgences that had at times even included opiate-based medication, Cobain felt heroin was on a different level and he began to lecture his friend about the risks and the overall impact the drug could have. Aside from the dangers, Cobain never envisioned heroin as an option for himself simply due to his fear of needles.

Despite Cobain's past views regarding heroin, physical and emotional changes curbed his position as the new decade began. Patterns of depression and a chronic stomach ailment, the former which increased following the dissolution of his relationship with Tobi Vail in November 1990, became unmanageable and impacted his artistic productivity.

In late 1990, clearly after overcoming his fear of needles, Cobain injected heroin for the first time. This timeline is not definitive and some research sources suggest Cobain's use of heroin occurred as early as 1987, though not necessarily intravenously. The euphoric high soothed his pains and he slowly developed an increasing pattern of use. Heroin, like other drugs in Cobain's past, acted as a form of self-medication; an escape both emotionally and physically. Soon after his initial use, Cobain confided in Novoselic who was alarmed and warned his friend of the risks associated with further heroin use. Novoselic specifically identified Andrew Wood as an example, the lead singer of the Seattle based band Mother Love Bone, who died of a heroin overdose in March 1990. At the time of Wood's death, Mother Love Bone was on the cusp of stardom with the July release of *Apple*, the band's major label debut. Unfortunately, Novoselic's warning to Cobain fell largely on deaf ears. Grohl, who still shared an apartment with Cobain, was equally concerned and confronted him. Cobain admitted that he had used heroin, but told Grohl he would not do it again. It was an assurance Cobain knew he could not keep. Ultimately, his relationship with his bandmates would never be the same following his admission. "We got disconnected," Novoselic later explained. "And a lot of it started with my objection to him doing heroin. He pushed me away after that. It was like I was some kind of scolding father."

The allure of heroin had become too powerful to Cobain. He eventually developed the rationale that if his chronic stomach ailment made him feel like an addict, he may as well become an addict and medicate himself. According to an undated journal entry, "I decided to use heroine (sic) on a daily basis because of an ongoing stomach ailment that I had been suffering from for the past five years had literally taken me to the point of wanting to kill myself. I bought a gun but chose drugs instead." As it became clear to Cobain that his bandmates would never agree with his heroin use, he began to use randomly and in secret. At times he disappeared for days, either locked inside his bedroom or secluded in seedy motel rooms scattered throughout King County. Over time, after numerous overdoses occurred and several detoxes proved unsuccessful, Cobain's opiate dependency led to friction with those closest to him. Eventually, most of his time outside the band was spent with other heroin addicts and those who turned a blind eye.

On New Year's Day, 1991, Nirvana returned to Seattle's Music Source studio for a brief session produced by the band's sound man, Craig Montgomery, who had always hoped to record the band. Because it was a holiday and Montgomery had an acquaintance who worked at Music Source, the band was not charged for studio time.

As the band had no commitments to Sub Pop and a new deal had not been signed elsewhere, the January session allowed for the opportunity to run through ideas and record prepared tracks. Among seven tracks that were recorded, the band completed "Aneurysm" and a re-recording of "Even In His Youth." Both tracks were used as B-sides in 1991 and would appear on the band's 1992 compilation, *Incesticide*. Early versions of "Drain You," "All Apologies," and "Radio Friendly Unit Shifter" were also recorded, all of which were eventually re-recorded and appeared on future albums. In March 1991, Cobain informed the *Backlash's* Dawn Anderson that the session did not go well and the Music Source was just "good for making Nordstrom commercials." The session was Grohl's first with the band and thus, in hindsight, that became the most memorable aspect of the Music Source session.

Coupled with the positive responses generated from their live shows and the moderate success of their debut album, as 1991 began Nirvana continued to attract interest from several major labels. Sub Pop hoped to secure the band for at least one year and presented a new thirty page contract, however Cobain was reluctant to sign. Additionally, due to cash strapped Sub Pop's desire to establish a partnership with a major label in hopes to act as a subsidiary, the band's aspiration to move on and cut out the proverbial "middle man" was heightened further.

At the recommendation of Soundgarden's manager, Susan Silver, Cobain and Novoselic traveled to Los Angeles to meet with Alan Mintz, an entertainment lawyer working with the firm Ziffren, Brittenham, and Branca. Mintz had a reputation for getting results and had represented several industry heavyweights, including the Rolling Stones and Kiss. He later described the pair as "naive but ambitious" and was alarmed at their appearance; attire that was far from conventional for a business meeting. Mintz also described that contrary to the impression his disheveled appearance presented, Cobain was earnest and career-minded regarding the band's motivation to transition from Sub Pop to a major label and eventually sell millions of records. Mintz was intrigued by their aspirations and agreed to take on Nirvana as clients in order to assist with the legal obstacles of a major label contract. He quickly began distributing the band's demo to several major labels which was compiled of several tracks recorded during the Smart Studios sessions. Additionally, to further assist with the inundation from labels, Nirvana signed with Gold Mountain Management, located in Los Angeles. Although Gold Mountain was not home to an ocean of indie artists, they had signed Sonic Youth who were viewed by many as the kings of the indie scene. Furthermore, Danny Goldberg, the founder of Gold Mountain, had been a publicist for Led Zeppelin in the mid-1970s. This nugget of information was enough to seal the deal between Nirvana and Gold Mountain.

Practice became routine as the band prepared material for their new album. A $1,000 monthly stipend, which was provided to each band member by Gold Mountain Entertainment while they continued to assess interest from major labels, allowed the band to focus on their upcoming album while Cobain wrote new music. "We were very disciplined and we took rehearsals and playing music seriously. There was really no messing around, no partying or having girls over or anything. It was very serious and we played the songs over and over again until we felt they sounded right and, you know, worked out all the bugs," Novoselic later described. With consistent income established, the immediacy of playing live for income was not necessary. As a result, Nirvana played less than ten shows during the first five months of 1991.

With eventual interest from at least eight major labels, Nirvana was in a position to bargain and negotiate any prospective contract. With the support of Mintz and Gold Mountain Entertainment, on April 30, 1991, the band signed with Geffen Records' imprint DGC Records. In exchange, the band received a $287,000 advance from Geffen Records, however taxes and various fees quickly decimated the sum.

Despite the relatively small advance, the band was in a position to earn millions if their next album exceeded gold status (500,000 units sold).

Along with the agreement, Geffen Records bought out Nirvana's contract from Sub Pop for $75,000. In addition, Sub Pop would receive two percent from sales for each of the band's two future albums. Long term, the buyout provided Sub Pop with millions. Compounded by their future financial link to Nirvana, following Bruce Pavitt's initial $20 investment to establish Sub Pop less than ten years prior, in 1995 Warner Brothers Records purchased 49% of the label's ownership stake for $20 million.

In late winter, as Cobain's output continued to generate strong material for their second album, he introduced a new riff to his bandmates, along with a chorus vocal melody. Though the band was not cognizant of its significance at the time, the riff would become one of the most famous in rock history. With input from both Novoselic and Grohl, the song was pieced together as a group resulting in a rarely shared writing credit. With the exception of a hidden track, the new track would become the only shared writing credit on the band's second album. "I was trying to write the ultimate pop song," Cobain acknowledged to *Rolling Stone* in 1994. "I was basically trying to rip off the Pixies. I have to admit it." The eventual song title, "Smells Like Teen Spirit," did not appear in the lyrics but was a phrase written randomly on Cobain's wall by Kathleen Hanna, Cobain's friend and the lead singer of the band Bikini Kill; "Kurt smells like Teen Spirit."

On April 17, and prior to embarking for California to begin work on their second album and reportedly coordinated last minute to secure enough gas money for the trek, Nirvana played a show with Bikini Kill and Fitz of Depression at Seattle's OK Hotel; a cultural landmark which was permanently affected when the Nisqually earthquake occurred in February 2001. Though not a sellout due to a party in the city the same night for the release of the movie *Singles*, the show proved to be a historical moment for Nirvana. Addressing the crowd early in the set, Cobain jokingly stated, "Hello, we're major label corporate rock sellouts." Several covers and previously released tracks encompassed the set, however toward the end of the show Cobain introduced the next song in their set by simply stating, "This song is called 'Smells Like Teen Spirit.'" By the song's second chorus the crowd's excitement was palpable. "The audience went nuts," Grohl later recalled. Unbeknownst to the band, although it was not yet completed, the song would be the catalyst in their eventual meteoritic rise. On that night the excitement created by the new song was undeniable, but within just two short years the mainstream's attraction to "Smells Like Teen Spirit" would become stifling for the band.

Though the timeframe of their initial introduction is debatable, and possibly occurring as early as 1989, by 1991 Courtney Love became a regular presence in the life of the Nirvana frontman. Two years Cobain's senior, Love was the lead singer and rhythm guitarist of the Los Angeles based band Hole whose debut album *Pretty on the Inside* was scheduled to be released that September. After his relationship with Tobi Vail ended, Cobain struggled with his self-worth more so than ever. Love's larger than life persona brought a new found excitement to Cobain's life, but not without toxicity.

Like Cobain, Love came from a broken home and spent her formative years relying on family members and friends for housing assistance. Her antics led to a placement at a juvenile detention center in Oregon at the age of fourteen after she was arrested for shoplifting. Friction with family members became routine and Love's lifestyle choices were unorthodox, including work acquired during her late teens as an exotic dancer. Over time, and with assistance from a small trust fund, Love settled in California and pursued a career in the entertainment industry. Her magnetic personality led to nearly instantaneous contacts and opportunities, including involvement in early incarnations of Faith No More followed by Babes In Toyland. In 1986, soon after securing a supporting role in the biopic *Sid and Nancy*, Love focused on music consistently. She taught herself the guitar and answered an ad in a Los Angeles periodical *The Recycler* seeking a bandmate who was interested in "Big Black, Sonic Youth, and Fleetwood Mac." Along with Eric Erlandson, the ad's author, a full band was recruited and by 1989 Hole was formed.

Love's initial pursuit of Cobain was obvious to many and, in the impression of some, overblown. In 1992, during an interview with *Sassy* magazine's Christina Kelly, Love acknowledged the lengths she went to win over Cobain. "I really pursued him. Not too aggressive, but aggressive enough that some girls would have been embarrassed by it."

After a period of uncertainty during the late winter, Nirvana settled on Butch Vig to produce their second album; the producer of the Smart Studios sessions one year prior. Vig had never worked with a major label, however his production work with Wisconsin based Killdozer had garnered acclaim. Shortly before the sessions were scheduled to begin in Los Angeles, Vig received a cassette in the mail from Cobain. Clearly recorded by the band on a boombox, the tape began with Cobain stating, "Hey Butch! We got a new drummer, his name's Dave Grohl, he's the best drummer in the world!" The band then launched into their newest track, "Smells Like Teen Spirit." Vig was left amazed and intrigued about what was to come.

In late April 1991, the band departed for Los Angeles. Novoselic and his wife drove separately in their Volkswagen bus, along with the band's equipment. Cobain and Grohl drove in Cobain's dated and rusted Datsun, however after less than an hour on the road the Datsun broke down. With little hope to complete the thousand mile journey in the dying vehicle, the pair were able to make the necessary repairs in order to return to Olympia. They then proceeded to hurl stones at the vehicle in frustration before departing for Los Angeles in the band's touring van.

All band members eventually arrived in Los Angeles unscathed and began three days of rehearsals before entering the studio. A rehearsal space was rented for the band in North Hollywood, along with fully furnished short-term rooms at the Oakwood Apartments for the duration of their stay in California. "We called it 'The Cokewoods' because it's where all the wannabe actors and rock bands stayed," Vig later recalled. The band quickly rearranged their rooms' furniture and added graffiti to the powder blue walls for a "like home" appeal.

Also residing temporarily at the Oakwood Apartments were members of the Swedish rock band Europe, known for the 1986 track "The Final Countdown." The band was recording in the city as well and planned to release their next album in September. Unbeknownst to Europe, their eventual album would receive very little media attention largely due to their temporary neighbors.

Within close proximity of the Oakwood Apartments, Sound City Studios had been secured as the production space for the new album. Located behind railroad tracks and among various warehouses, Sound City Studios had become somewhat rundown since originally opening in 1969. Despite its appearance in 1991, during the two previous decades the studio had been an epicenter for album production. Several classic albums had been produced at Sound City Studios, evidence of which was hung in the form of album covers on the hallway walls, including Fleetwood Mac's *Fleetwood Mac*, Neil Young's *After the Goldrush*, and Tom Petty's *Damn the Torpedoes*. Additional studio clients included Ronnie James Dio, Foreigner, and the Jackson 5. Cobain was largely unimpressed with the studio's history until he learned that a childhood hero, Evel Knievel, had recorded the album *Evel Speaks to the Kids* at the studio. In addition to its history, Sound City Studios was home to the Neve 8028; a rare analog mixing console designed and manufactured by Neve Electronics. Twenty years later, after Sound City Studios was closed by its original owners, the same Neve 8028 used by

Nirvana in 1991 was purchased by Grohl and moved into his own studio; Studio 606. "It doesn't change the performance but it does enhance the way that it sounds," Grohl described to NPR in 2013. "You know, it's the difference between listening to an old record on an old stereo versus listening to something off of your iPod."

On May 2, Nirvana began basic recording at Sound City Studios. With a $65,000 budget and stellar material, all parties anticipated a positive outcome. The main studio used during the sessions was the largest the band had ever recorded in, but the trio's power filled every inch. Due to the band's strict commitment to routine rehearsals, all songs designated for the album were prepared and ready for the sessions, with Grohl adopting many of Chad Channing's drum grooves from songs written prior to the Smart Studios sessions in 1990. Each day the band worked eight to ten hours and started every session with a jam; a format which produced many songs throughout their career. Typically, Vig would arrive around noon to prepare the studio and the band would show up mid-afternoon and work until around midnight. "We'd work from like noon and then we'd go to Venice Beach at night to see the sun come up," Novoselic later recalled. "It was a magical time. We were carefree, we were on top of the world, making the music we wanted to make - we were having fun."

Similar to his methods during the recording of *Bleach*, Cobain had not finished the lyrics to several of the songs which were to be featured on their second album until the recording sessions had begun - and in some cases, moments prior. "We were just standing there with our arms crossed and our feet tapping, just staring at Kurt as he sat there sweating and writing and looking and writing and looking," Novoselic recalled to *The Rocket* in 1991.

Grohl's influence on the band's live performances had become immediately evident, however his presence in the studio was equally as significant. Vig recalled the importance of Grohl's addition to Nirvana and his impact on the band's second album years later. "He's the best drummer I know, hands down. He really locked Chris and Kurt together; those songs are really powerful and a lot of that has to do with his drumming because he's just *on* it."

Tracks completed during the Smart Studios sessions, but re-recorded at Sound City, included "Breed" (formerly known as "Immodium"), "Lithium," and "Stay Away" (also known as "Pay To Play"). The only recording carried over from the Smart Studios sessions for inclusion on the band's second album was "Polly," including Channing's original cymbal crashes. The acoustic track was based on the 1987 kidnapping and rape of a fourteen-year-old Washington girl by Gerald Arthur Friend. After being held captive by Friend and tortured with a blow torch, among other methods, the child was eventually able to escape. Friend was captured soon after and later sentenced to serve a seventy-five-year period of incarceration.

Following the dissolution of his relationship with Tobi Vail, Cobain used songwriting to cope, among other methods. Two songs recorded during the sessions, and written about his relationship with Vail, included "Drain You" and "Lounge Act." Vail had entered Cobain's life at an impressionable time, resulting in several scattered references throughout the album.

Written by Cobain in 1990, "Something In the Way" was originally intended to be performed by the full band at the Sound City sessions. Initial attempts to record the song with the band were unsuccessful and failed to grasp the song's underlying depth and heartache. Utilizing a modified twelve string guitar, purchased for $20 one year prior in Denver, Colorado, Cobain eventually laid down on the control room floor and performed a solo rendition of the song for Vig. The producer later recalled that he hurriedly turned off the studio's phones, every fan, and held his breath for fear that the slightest noise would spoil the fragile recording. "His performance stunned me," Vig described years later. "He had gone deep inside himself and brought out a haunting portrait of desolation, weariness, and paranoia." To provide further depth to the song's beauty and simplicity, on one of the session's final days, a cello was added by a friend of the band, Kirk Canning.

Overall, fifteen tracks were recorded in sixteen days, and typically in just two or three takes. Although their power had carried over during the Sound City sessions, the band was initially critical of the final rough mixes completed at Devonshire Sound Studios. In an effort to seek fresh ears, DGC provided a list of possible producer / engineers and the band settled on Andy Wallace - the co-producer of Slayer's *Seasons In the Abyss*. The prospect of Wallace excited Cobain, not solely due to his work with Slayer, but more so because he was not significantly known. Completed by Wallace on June 10, the final mix thrilled the band and the greatest impact was felt on the guitar and drum sounds. Throughout the final mix, irresistible hooks could be heard on nearly every track which detailed symbolism contrary to many of the largely hedonistic rock songs on mainstream radio and being performed in most arenas.

Mastering was completed on August 2 at the Mastering Lab, located in Hollywood and the final track list included: "Smells Like Teen Spirit," "In Bloom," "Come As You Are," "Breed" (formerly Immodium), "Lithium," "Polly," "Territorial Pissings," "Drain You," "Lounge Act," "Stay Away" (also known as "Pay to Play"), "On a Plain," and "Something In the Way." "Sappy" (also known as "Verse Chorus Verse") and "Old Age" were recorded during the sessions, but not included on the album. Each track was eventually released on future compilations. A hidden track, titled "Endless, Nameless," appeared 13 minutes and 51 seconds following the last note of "Something In the Way" and at approximately 19 minutes and 32 seconds Cobain could be heard smashing his guitar to bits. Unfortunately, the track was left off of 50,000 initial pressings of the album due to a simple error at the Mastering Lab. Overall, unexpected production needs ballooned total costs to $120,000 to $130,000. A recoup for the label was not initially a given. Regardless, the punk/pop format had been perfected and several tracks on the album were believed to be possible singles including "Lithium," "In Bloom," "On a Plain," and "Come As You Are." Ultimately, the band settled on "Smells Like Teen Spirit" as their first single.

Despite the universal praise many of the tracks would receive, Cobain became the album's biggest critic. "Looking back on the production of *Nevermind,* I'm embarrassed by it now," he acknowledged. "It's closer to a Motley Crue record than it is a punk record." Cobain felt he was viewed as a hypocrite and a traitor who was comfortable surrendering his artistic values for commercial acceptance. It was a battle his psyche would fight for the remainder of his short life.

Nirvana's laborious journey to complete their major label debut was approaching a completion, however additional work was needed. Until then, in mid-June the band began a two-week trek of the West Coast with Dinosaur Jr. who were touring in support of their own release, *Green Mind.* Still two months away from the release of their major label debut, Nirvana had begun to play new tracks off of the album live at each tour stop. Slowly, a reaction to the tracks was being felt from fans with every passing show.

Soon after the completion of the tour, Grohl moved out of the apartment he had shared with Cobain for nearly one year. Grohl's departure had little impact on Cobain who was slowly beginning to spend most free days using heroin and nodding off alone. His promises to stop using were broken. A physical and emotional dependency had begun.

Adding to Cobain's struggles, following a brief trip to California in late July to complete promotional photos for the album, he returned to Olympia and discovered that he had been evicted. His worldly possessions, including his journals, had been carelessly piled up on the sidewalk outside the apartment, just bordering the street. Cobain's beloved turtles were missing, after being sold several weeks prior for financial assistance. For over three years, the North Pear Street apartment had served as an escape for Cobain, providing him the isolation he sought. Slim Moon, Cobain's friend and North Pear Street neighbor, described him as a "hermit in a cave" who would "play his guitar for twelve hours a day and never leave his house except to go on tour." Many songs had been crafted, written, and rewritten within the small apartment. Perhaps no location served Cobain's artistic output better. Oh, if those walls could talk!

As work continued to finalize the album, Cobain and Grohl watched a documentary on water births. An intriguing idea arose and the band proposed a tentative album cover featuring a baby underwater. The full scope of the idea was sketched out by Cobain and a photo shoot for the album cover was coordinated soon after. Four sets of parents arrived at the shoot, along with their infant children; both male and female. Five-month-old Spencer Elden was chosen and his underwater photo, captured while naked, was used for the cover. A fish hook with a dollar bill, just out of the baby's grasp, was shot afterwards and superimposed onto the photo. The finished album cover became iconic and to the surprise of the band and their label, very little censorship was sought by retail stores following the album's release. In California, a resident took umbrage with the album's cover which had been perched in a record store window. A simple Post-It note was used to alleviate the dispute. In 2021, Elden filed suit against the band claiming that the album's cover was child pornography and the band profited off of his trafficked image. The suit was dismissed soon thereafter.

In preparation for the release of *Nevermind*'s first single, flyers were distributed on August 15 during a showcase event at the Roxy Theatre inviting attendees to be extras two days later at the video shoot for "Smells Like Teen Spirit." Extras between the ages of eighteen and twenty-five were encouraged to "adapt a high school personna (sic), i.e., preppy, punk, nerd, jock." The idea for the video was conceived by Cobain and loosely based on films he held dear, including *Over the Edge* and *Rock and Roll High School*. Every shot was sketched out by Cobain in advance and a budget of $50,000 was allocated for its completion.

On August 17, at GMT Studios, located in Culver City, California, the video for "Smells Like Teen Spirit" was filmed on a set constructed to resemble a dilapidated gymnasium and featured a high school pep rally, cheerleaders, the band, and concluded in an eruption of pure anarchy; essentially a scene of chaos and passion found at an average Nirvana performance. Upon its release, the video received critical acclaim and debuted on MTV's *120 Minutes* before transitioning within two weeks to the channel's "Buzz Bin," which guaranteed that it would be broadcast numerous times per day.

9

THE STORM

On September 24, 1991, Nirvana released their second studio album titled *Nevermind*. Initially planning to name the album *Sheep*, the band chose *Nevermind* reportedly as a metaphor for Cobain's attitude toward life. The album was preempted by the release of "Smells Like Teen Spirit" to radio on August 27 and for sale as a single on September 10. As early as Labor Day weekend, essentially three days after it's release, "Smells Like Teen Spirit" had begun to show a steady increase in airplay on many nationwide radio stations. Despite the song's nearly instantaneous popularity, initially DGC did not have profound expectations for *Nevermind* and estimated that the album would sell less than 100,000 copies. As a result, only 46,251 copies of *Nevermind* were shipped to stores within the United States and 35,000 copies were shipped to stores within the United Kingdom. Following the album's release, despite an initial scarcity, it debuted at number 144 on the Billboard 200 and sold 6,000 copies in its first week. A fire had been lit.

Reviews were largely positive for *Nevermind* both in the United States and England: *The New York Times* - "With *Nevermind*, Nirvana has certainly succeeded. There are enough intriguing textures, mood shifts, instrumental snippets and inventive word plays to provide for hours of entertainment." *Rolling Stone* - "A dynamic mix of sizzling power chords, manic energy and sonic restraint, Nirvana erects melodic structures - sing-along hard rock as defined by groups like the Replacements, Pixies and Sonic Youth - but then attacks them with frenzied screaming and guitar havoc." *New Musical Express* - "*Nevermind* is the big American alternative record of the autumn. But better still, it'll last well into next year." *Melody Maker* - "When Nirvana released *Bleach* all those years ago, the more sussed among us figured they had the potential to make an album that would blow every other contender away. My God, they have proved us right."

One month before the release of *Nevermind*, on August 20, 1991, Nirvana embarked on a brief overseas festival tour supporting Sonic Youth, which also featured performances by Dinosaur Jr., the Ramones, Gumball, and Babes In Toyland. The tour was filmed entirely on a Super 8 camera by Dave Markey, a friend of Sonic Youth, and resulted in the documentary *1991: The Year Punk Broke*. The all-access footage provided a glimpse of the catalyst which was just weeks from changing the music industry. During the tour Nirvana were routinely the standouts amongst stellar lineups, but the moment that stood out to many was the band's approximate 40 minute performance to an elated crowd of thousands on August 23 at the Reading Music Festival, located in Reading, England. Despite the early 2:00 P.M. appearance on the bill, sandwiched between sets by largely unknown acts Silverfish and Chapterhouse, Nirvana's raw and visceral set was palpable. Many songs from *Bleach* were performed, along with tracks which would be released on *Nevermind* one month later. The set also included "Tony the Interpretive Dancer" shirtless and flailing about between Cobain and Novoselics, a guest appearance by the Vaselines' Eugene Kelly for a performance of "Molly's Lips," and concluded with "Endless, Nameless." Following the destruction of the band's equipment, Cobain launched himself into Grohl's drum set, resulting in a dislocated shoulder. Moments later he rose and waved to the adoring audience as he left the stage. A review of the set, featured in the October edition of the British magazine *Raw!* summarized what everyone at the show felt: "Then came a shock. Nirvana were mind blowing. Band of the day, and no mistake."

In Toronto, on September 20, three weeks after returning from Europe, and just four days prior to the release of *Nevermind*, Nirvana began a North American tour in support of the album's release. In 1993, Cobain described the tour to David Fricke of *Rolling Stone*. "The best times were right when *Nevermind* was coming out and we went on that American tour where we were playing clubs. They were totally sold out, and the record was breaking big, and there was this massive feeling in the air, this vibe of energy."

Following Nirvana's Canadian leg of the tour, which consisted of two shows, the band flew from Montreal to Boston. On September 22, with a rare night off, the band ventured to see the Melvins at the Rathskeller, commonly referred to in the city as "The Rat." After the band was turned away at the door, a young woman intervened and informed the doorman that Nirvana would be playing the

WFNX Birthday Bash in the city the following night. Once he was inside the club, Cobain thanked the woman, who introduced herself as Mary Lou Lord; a local musician and busker. A conversation ensued and Cobain was immediately taken by Lord's vast musical interests, which largely mirrored his own. Lord was amazed Cobain knew many of the largely unknown musicians she mentioned, including Daniel Johnston, Teenage Fanclub, and the Vaselines. Later that night, Cobain accepted a ride to his hotel from Lord only to discover her unlocking a bicycle near the front of the club. Hesitant for a moment, Cobain was swayed when Lord stated firmly, "Get on the back."

The pair spent the following day together, walking to various record stores throughout Boston before Nirvana's show that night at the Axis Nightclub. At the club, Cobain held Lord's hand and introduced her to an acquaintance as his girlfriend. Later in the week, at Cobain's insistence, Lord traveled to New York City where it became clear a relationship was forming. On September 29, along with very few others, the pair waited patiently in Cobain's room at the Roger Smith Hotel for the world premiere of the "Smells Like Teen Spirit" music video on MTV's *120 Minutes*. Lord remained by Cobain's side during several subsequent shows, however she was eventually forced to return to Boston for fear that she would lose her job.

On October 12, the band returned to Chicago's Cabaret Metro for an energetic set where Cobain was met by Courtney Love. Although their relationship had not yet been declared, Love had been a sporadic presence in Cobain's life throughout 1991. Following the band's set, Love made her way backstage and soon onto Cobain's lap. His attraction to Love had grown and the pair soon made their way back to the Days Inn where they had sex for the first time. Although Cobain adored Mary Lou Lord, along with his exes Tracy Marander and Tobi Vail, Love understood Cobain and he understood her. The pair had a similar background and shared a passion for music, but they soon shared another commonality.

On October 24, Hole opened for Nirvana in Tijuana. Although Cobain and Love had kept in touch over the phone, it was the first time the pair had seen each other since Chicago. The following night, the two bands played the Rock for Choice benefit in Los Angeles. After the show, the pair retired to Cobain's hotel room, had sex, and they both injected heroin. As a recovering addict Love was hesitant to use again, however Cobain was insistent that the pair share the experience and he eventually injected her dose.

Any uncertainty Mary Lou Lord had developed regarding her relationship with Cobain was confirmed when, on November 8 during the live television broadcast of "The Word," Cobain grabbed the microphone before the band's performance of "Smells Like Teen Spirit" and stated, "I'd like all of you people in this room to know that Courtney Love, of the sensational pop group Hole, is the best fuck in the world." His relationship with Lord had ended as quickly as it had begun.

Cobain's relationship with Love had become a freight train and driven, albeit initially, by a mutual pattern of heroin abuse. In 1992, Love acknowledged the impact created by narcotics and described that she and Cobain "bonded over pharmaceuticals." Within four months, Cobain and Love became expectant parents and were married, but contrary to the typical happiness a young family may experience media accounts painted a scene of disorder fueled by addiction and manipulation. By early 1994, a divorce seemed possible and, to some, inevitable. "Kurt Cobain is regarded as a holy man. Courtney, meanwhile, is viewed by many as a charismatic opportunist," journalist Lynn Hirschberg summarized in 1992. "Where Courtney projects strength, Kurt seems fragile. He looks as if he might break." It was Hirschberg's *Vanity Fair* article detailing Love's possible heroin use while pregnant that proved to be the catalyst leading to the brief removal of the couple's daughter later the same year, shortly after the child's birth.

From coast to coast during the fall tour, the electricity generated by Nirvana at each show had become infectious. At some venues, fans filling the streets hoping to get inside rivaled the sum that held tickets. Attendees routinely described shows of pure adrenaline and celebration. Cobain and Novoselic continued to destroy their equipment on a routine basis and, at times, Grohl followed suit. Stages were left in disarray. "Every time we played, it was blood and guts," Grohl declared in 2019.

At times, attendance within venues dangerously exceeded the legal capacity. Such was the case on October 19, at the Trees Club in Dallas, Texas, during the band's performance of "Love Buzz," when Cobain jumped into the crowd but the tightly packed room caused him to fall back toward the stage. As a bouncer tried somewhat aggressively to pull Cobain back, his head met the butt end of Cobain's guitar. With blood pouring from his head, the bouncer punched Cobain in the head and then kicked him in the torso as the lead singer fell to the ground. Novoselic immediately dropped his bass and came to his friend's defense, confronting the bouncer while removing his shirt in a taunting manner, as the crowd erupted. Once the scene calmed, following chants of "bullshit" from the audience over fears that the show would be cut short, the band returned to the stage. Clearly unsettled by the incident, Cobain stated to the audience, "I must apologize for all the violence." The band then segued into "Pennyroyal Tea" and played for another twenty minutes before finishing the set. Fearful of retribution, the band was then ushered quickly out of the building to a waiting taxi. Despite the efforts to avoid further violence, the bouncer advanced toward the taxi and punched a hole through a side window as the vehicle sped off into the night.

Following the chaos in Dallas, Nirvana performed on nine of the subsequent eleven days, including shows in Houston, Austin, Tempe, Los Angeles, and Vancouver. Rest was infrequent as promotion was integral between shows during the initial weeks following the release of *Nevermind*. On October 25, Cobain and Novoselic appeared on MTV's *Headbangers Ball*. Somewhat ambivalent about appearing on a show that had gained its popularity during the rise of hair metal, Cobain arrived wearing an unsavory yellow ball gown with a ridiculously large and flowing collar. While also wearing sunglasses and appearing bored, Cobain voiced his frustration with Novoselic during the broadcast for not wearing his tuxedo or getting the singer a corsage for "the ball." The show's host, Riki Rachtman, observed the exchange in bewilderment. Cobain said little else during the appearance and relied on Novoselic to converse with Rachtman.

The North American tour culminated in a homecoming show on Halloween at Seattle's Paramount Theatre, with the band's family and friends in attendance. With significant demand and the prospect of greater ticket sales, the show was moved just days prior from the Moore Theatre to the larger Paramount Theatre. Although Mudhoney was planned as the show's headliner, the public's enormous response to *Nevermind* could not be ignored - Nirvana headlined. During the iconic Halloween show, the bright lights caused shadows of the three musicians to be cast in grand scale along the theatre walls. Additionally, Ian Dickson and Nikki McClure acted as go-go dancers in comedic fashion on stage while wearing shirts; his stating "girl" and hers stating "boy." Their presence added to the chaotic scene which ended in traditional fashion as the band smashed their equipment following "Endless, Nameless." The performance was filmed by a crew financed by Geffen Records in what would eventually be viewed as one of the greatest performances of Nirvana's career.

Less than one week later, Nirvana began a European tour in support of *Nevermind*. Shortly following the band's arrival in England, and just six weeks after the album's release, *Nevermind* had surged into the top 50 albums on the Billboard 200. Meanwhile, "Smells Like Teen Spirit" topped the Modern Rock chart soon after. For one month the band took over Europe in a frenzied scene of adoration, including shows in London, Berlin, Vienna, Rome, and Amsterdam. On December 6, shortly prior to the conclusion of the European tour, Nirvana appeared on the British television show *Tonight With Jonathan Ross* and were introduced as "the biggest band in the world right now." Upon returning to the United States soon after, the band members briefly went their separate ways and quickly discovered that things would never be the same.

Cobain began to struggle internally with the paradox created by his little punk band selling hundreds of thousands of albums. He was embarrassed by his success and any presumption of ostentatious behavior. Although his wife was comfortable with glamour, Cobain chose to drive an aged vehicle and wore second hand clothes. Equally troubling for Cobain was the shift in the band's fanbase at shows. The once largely liberal audience began to include overly macho jocks; the same men who would have taunted him in high school. "It just made me feel so stupid because there are so many other bands in the underground that are as good or better than we are and we're the only ones getting the attention," Cobain later described. "But, I knew that it was better than ninety-nine percent of anything else on a commercial level."

On October 29, just one month after the release *Nevermind*, the album was certified gold and soon entered the Top 40 of the Billboard 200. As a result of the high demand, *Nevermind* was sold out at many record stores throughout the United States during the initial weeks following its release. Copies in the United Kingdom were equally as scarce and duplicates dubbed onto cassettes became common place. In order to meet the public's astonishing demand for the album,

Geffen Records briefly suspended factory production of all the label's artists' compact discs and focused solely on the production of *Nevermind*. Throughout the fall of 1991 the sales of *Nevermind* grew exponentially at a rate on average of 300,000 copies per week and by the New Year the album had sold two million copies. During the last week of December, *Nevermind* sold 373,250 copies largely as a result of teens spending their Christmas cash and gift certificates on the most popular album in the world. It was also widely reported that many albums received as Christmas gifts were returned following the holiday in exchange for a copies of *Nevermind*. Throughout the next twelve months, album sales remained consistently high due to continued word of mouth and the release of superb singles and music videos for "Come As You Are," "Lithium," and "In Bloom."

On January 10, 1992, Nirvana performed at MTV Studios in New York City. The distinctive setting included a second story walkway at the rear of the stage which allowed fans to drape their legs just above Grohl's flailing sticks as chaotic stage lights of varying colors flooded the band throughout the set. In addition to the stage design, Cobain's hair, dyed Kool Aid red days prior, added to the unique visual. The taped show was broadcast soon after and featured several tracks from *Nevermind* including "Smells Like Teen Spirit," "Polly," "On a Plain," and "Drain You."

The following day, and somewhat poetically, after *Nevermind* outsold commercial titans Michael Jackson, Garth Brooks, Hammer, and U2, the album replaced Jackson's *Dangerous* as the number one album on the Billboard 200 chart. The same day, in a moment of zeitgeist, Nirvana performed "Smells Like Teen Spirit" and "Territorial Pissings" on one of the few remaining benchmarks of American music and comedy, *Saturday Night Live*. A band from a quiet logging town in the middle of nowhere, and largely unknown just three years prior, had conquered the music industry and paved the way for a sea change.

Although the band's accomplishments were cause for celebration, Cobain's increasing heroin addiction was evident to most during the weeks prior to the band's *Saturday Night Live* performance and quickly became the media's focus. Though he was always thin, Cobain had become frail, overly pale, and, on occasion, he would nod off. *BAM*, a California based music paper, published one of the first articles referencing Cobain's apparent drug abuse in January 1992. "He's had but an hour's sleep, he says blearily," noted journalist Jerry McCulley in the article when describing his December 27, 1991, interview with the lead singer. "But the pinned pupils; sunken cheeks; and scabbed, sallow skin suggest something more serious than mere fatigue." Sadly, but somewhat fitting, as the *Saturday Night Live* cast and guests waved good night as the credits rolled, Cobain shook hands and stood by comedian Chris Farley; another once in a generation talent whose internal struggles were compounded by the grip of addiction.

Following the show, Cobain fled from Studio 8H, skipping the traditional after party, and retired to his hotel room after a lengthy interview with disc jockey and author, Kurt St. Thomas. He was focused and one priority had surpassed all others. Seated and concentrating solely on the needle, Cobain led the mainline to the vein which was followed by an almost immediate loss of consciousness. Several hours later, Love awoke to discover Cobain lying nearby, appearing lifeless. He had overdosed. Love quickly threw cold water on his body and punched him repeatedly in the stomach. An eventual gasp was heard. Cobain had survived.

10

THE LEGACY

Nevermind maintained a consistent position on the Billboard 200 for months following its release and, per the Recording Industry Association of America, by the end of the 20th century the album had sold over ten million copies. As a result of Nirvana's initial popularity and success, major labels developed a tidal wave of interest in "alternative" artists with the hope that the second coming of Nirvana was a possibility. Over time, many of Nirvana's peers were signed to major labels, including TAD, Mudhoney, the Melvins, and the Butthole Surfers. In early 1992, less than three years after their formation, New York based Helmet was signed by Interscope for $1 million. Just six months prior, major labels would not return the band's calls. Nirvana's influence also carried over to a generation of new bands, many of which provided the soundtrack throughout the remainder of the 90s and into the 21st century, including Oasis, Green Day, Weezer, Silverchair, and Bush.

Within two years of Nirvana's breakthrough, Geffen Records grossed an astounding $50 million. In order to further capitalize on Nirvana's worth, Geffen purchased several of the band's unreleased and previously released songs from Sub Pop for a compilation release. As part of the agreement and distribution plan, the band would create and approve of the release by the end of 1992. Cobain was enticed further by the prospect of having complete control of the album's artwork. Ultimately, the cover featured art painted by Cobain and on December 14, 1992, *Incesticide* was released. Featuring fifteen tracks that had been recorded sporadically with four different drummers between January 1988 and November 1991, *Incesticide* provided an overview of Nirvana's evolution. The album included previously unreleased tracks "Big Long Now," "Aero Zeppelin," and "Hairspray Queen," previously released tracks "Sliver," "Dive," and "Stain," and alternate versions of previously released tracks "Been a Son," "(New Wave) Polly," and "Aneurysm." Within just two months, an album composed largely of B-sides sold 500,000 copies.

On September 21, 1993, nearly two years after the release of their breakthrough, Nirvana released their third and final studio album titled *In Utero*. Following a tumultuous first half of 1992 due to the severity of Cobain's drug addiction, stalled touring, media scrutiny, and threats of a breakup, the band stabilized and headlined England's Reading Festival in August; a performance considered by many to be a career highlight. Ten days later, a rollicking performance at MTV's annual Video Music Awards further enlivened the trio. With both old and new compositions available, some tracks which were initially attempted on tape as early as 1990, production plans for the third album began in October. Planned as a purposeful deviation from the polished production of *Nevermind*, *In Utero* was also an attempt by the band to return to their punk influenced roots. Novoselic later described the material as "a litmus test towards our audience."

Recording engineer Steve Albini was chosen by the band as the producer of their third album due to his unique recording techniques and indie credentials. Albini accepted a flat fee of $100,000 to complete the task and refused to accept any future royalties. Recorded during a two week period in February 1993 at the snow-covered Pachyderm Studios, located just outside the small town of Cannon Falls, Minnesota, *In Utero* contained Cobain's most personal compositions, several of which told stories related to his past, present, and future. The isolated locale was chosen in an effort to deter media attention and limit Cobain's risk of relapse. Additionally, the band slept and ate at an adjoining house and were essentially cut off from the world during production. To further hide their presence, the band was booked at Pachyderm Studios as The Simon Ritchie Bluegrass Ensemble. All songs were recorded live and completed in six days, while mixing took an additional five days. Sessions were completed on February 26 and described as uneventful and, at times, humorous until Courtney Love arrived seven days into production and created an environment of tension. Her hostile presence earned her the term "psycho hose-beast" by Albini.

Although DGC took issue with the raw and abrasive final recording, resulting in remixes of presumed singles, *In Utero* ultimately debuted at number one on both sides of the Atlantic, eventually selling over five million copies in the United States alone. Tracks such as "Serve the Servants," "Heart Shaped Box," "Rape Me," "Dumb," "Pennyroyal Tea," and "All Apologies" proved Cobain's genius once again. Some later dissected the album, which had the working title *I Hate Myself and I Want To Die*, and believe in hindsight that the lyrics were hints and references to Cobain's emotional stress and all too brief future. While *Nevermind* will always be considered the band's commercial success, *In Utero* has become recognized as Nirvana's uncompromising masterpiece for its strength and vulnerability.

On November 18, 1993, as part of MTV's popular "Unplugged" series, Nirvana performed an enchanting acoustic set at Sony Studios in New York City in front of a live crowd surrounding the stage. The stage setting was designed largely by Cobain and included black candles and an ocean of white lilies; a flower believed to represent rebirth and purity. When he requested candles, flowers, and even a chandelier hanging over head, the show's producer inquired, "Like a funeral?" "Yes, exactly," Cobain affirmed. The show opened with "About a Girl," but not before Cobain passively stated, "This is off our first record, most people don't own it." Performing with 1993 and 1994 touring guitarist, Pat Smear, and cellist, Lori Goldston, the band's fourteen song set was a mix of covers and originals from each studio album, along with a guest appearance by the Meat Puppets. The approximate one hour performance was filmed in one take and captured Nirvana's unassuming beauty and depth. The subsequent album of the recording, titled *MTV Unplugged in New York*, was released on November 1, 1994, and debuted at number one on the Billboard 200. Universal praise followed and eventually earned the band their only Grammy award and has since sold over eight million copies in the United States.

Following the release of *In Utero*, Nirvana began a tour of arenas throughout North America and Europe. Concluding their twenty-three song set with "Heart Shaped

Box" and a surge of feedback, Nirvana's final concert appearance occurred on March 1, 1994, at the Terminal Einz in Munich, Germany. The venue was nothing more than a repurposed airplane hanger with poor acoustics for the approximate 3,000 fans in attendance. The resulting sound was regrettable and, in hindsight, an unfortunate conclusion to one of the greatest live acts of the late 20th century. Pale and struggling with laryngitis and bronchitis, Cobain's performance was admirable given his condition and ended with the frontman graciously stating, "Goodnight. Thank you." As a result of Cobain's physical condition, the remaining dates of the European tour were cancelled. He never performed again.

Three days later, after ingesting approximately fifty Rohypnol pills at Rome's Hotel Excelsior, Cobain fell into a coma. He had been found by his wife, on the brink of death. In his left hand, Cobain held a suicide note: "Like Hamlet, I have to choose between life and death. I choose death." Cobain quickly stabilized and later claimed the incident was accidental. On March 8, soon after being transferred from the Policlinico Umberto Primo to the Rome American Hospital, Cobain was discharged and he returned to Seattle. The subsequent month became a chaotic quest to save Cobain from himself, which included a drug intervention, Police responses, a hired Private Investigator, and hope.

Within twenty-eight months of *Nevermind's* unexpected triumph on the Billboard chart, and Nirvana's subsequent worldwide stardom, twenty-seven-year-old Kurt Cobain would be dead from a self-inflicted shotgun blast at his home in Seattle. After absconding from the Exodus Recovery Center in Los Angeles on April 1, 1994, where he had been admitted just two days prior to address his heroin addiction, Cobain returned to Seattle. Few saw him during the ensuing days before he barricaded himself inside the second story greenhouse above the garage at his Lake Washington home, injected heroin, and took his own life. His body was discovered on the morning of April 8 by an electrician who had arrived at the home to install a security system. Before the police were notified, the electrician's colleague contacted Seattle's KXRX radio with the exclusive story. Within the hour, news outlets around the world were reporting on Cobain's death. It was estimated that Cobain's death had occurred three days prior. A 20-gauge shotgun was found lying partially across his chest. A wallet had been opened and laid out nearby with Cobain's Washington State driver's license visible; conveniently providing the decedent's identification for emergency personnel. A conclusive identification was only obtained from fingerprints.

An increasing heroin dependency, domestic instability, and the stressors of fame had proven to be too much - Nirvana was over. Cobain, who would ultimately be referred to as "the voice of a generation," left behind a wife, their daughter, and millions of devoted fans. A suicide note, addressed to his imaginary friend from childhood, "Boddah," was left just feet from his body and summarized his frustrations with the life thrust upon him for no other reason than is own talents. It concluded with the phrase: "I don't have the passion anymore, and so remember, it's better to burn out than to fade away."

A vigil was held for fans near the Space Needle in Seattle on April 10, while a private service was held nearby for 150 invited guests. Reverend Stephen Towles officiated the service and equated suicide to the anguish of a slowly closing vice. "The pain becomes so great that you can't bear it any longer." Cobain's body was not present. He would be cremated soon after.

A final ceremony for Cobain took place on Memorial Day in 1999 behind his mother's new home in Olympia. During the brief service, Courtney Love, Cobain's mother and father, Tracy Marander, and others watched as six-year-old Frances Bean Cobain scattered her father's ashes into McLane Creek; a source which enters Puget Sound south of Seattle before eventually emptying into the Pacific Ocean.

Nirvana, LLC., was established soon after Cobain's death in order for Nirvana's music to be jointly managed by the band members and Cobain's family. Unfortunately, since 1994, internal battles have deterred the timely release of the band's unheard work. In 2002, following uncertainty regarding a proper distribution strategy, "You Know You're Right" was released as part of a best of compilation titled *Nirvana*. The song was recorded on January 30, 1994, at Robert Lang Studios, in Seattle, during a session which would prove to be the band's last. The master tapes were stored in Novoselic's basement where they remained into the next decade. "I kept it safe. I kept it like a secret," Novoselic described to *Rolling Stone* in 2002. Upon release, the song received universal praise and eventually topped the Billboard mainstream and modern rock charts. *Entertainment Weekly* noted that "Even in a genre that continues to be degraded by imitators, Cobain's rusty-piped voice and painful sarcasm are so raw it's scary."

In 2014, the band's first year of eligibility, Nirvana was inducted into the Rock and Roll Hall of Fame. The ceremony was held in New York City amongst an audience of thousands, including family members, friends, industry juggernauts, and fans. Nirvana was inducted by friend and lead singer of the band R.E.M., Michael Stipe. During his speech, Stipe stated, "Lyrically exposing our frailty, our frustrations, our shortcomings. Singing of retreat and acceptance over triumphs of an outsider community with such immense possibility, stymied or ignored, but not held down or held back by the stupidity and political pettiness of the times. They spoke truth, and a lot of people listened." The night culminated with Krist Novoselic, Dave Grohl, and Pat Smear, joined onstage by Lorde, Joan Jett, St. Vincent, and Sonic Youth's Kim Gordon; each female vocalist taking the stage separately to sing lead on Nirvana tracks which included "Smells Like Teen Spirit," "Lithium," "Aneurysm," and "All Apologies."

Now in the digital age, fans have found new ways to experience Nirvana. As of 2024, Nirvana has averaged thirty million monthly listeners on the streaming service Spotify. Furthermore, "Smells Like Teen Spirit" alone has been streamed on Spotify nearly two billion times. Traditional formats remain and, according to Nielsen Music, four of the top ten songs played on mainstream rock radio from 2010 to 2019 were Nirvana songs: "Smells Like Teen Spirit," "Come As You Are," "In Bloom," and "Lithium." Overall, with the release of three studio albums, twenty-one singles, five live albums, and four compilation albums, Nirvana has sold approximately 75 million albums worldwide.

Following Cobain's death his bandmates pursued varying musical careers and interests, but have always remained close to each other and loyal to their fallen friend. Krist Novoselic, greying and now slightly reserved, transitioned to various musical endeavors and bands, including Sweet 75, Eyes Adrift, Flipper, and Giants In Trees. Additionally, having maintained an interest in politics throughout his adult life, Novoselic supported numerous campaigns in the State of Washington and formed the Joint Artists and Music Promotions Political Action Committee (JAMPAC), a proactive organization that advocated on behalf of the music community. Novoselic and Shelli Dilley were divorced in 1999, he eventually remarried, and now resides on a farm in a small town in Washington, along with two children. As a cathartic release following his friend's death, in October 1994, Dave Grohl recorded a demo containing new material. Each of the fifteen tracks were written and recorded solely by Grohl, apart from a brief appearance by the Afghan Whigs' guitarist Greg Dulli. He eventually chose to recruit a full band followed by the release of a debut album in 1995. Novoselic was invited to join the newly formed band, however he and Grohl decided to avoid the emotional impact it could have created. Grohl's new band was christened the Foo Fighters and it became one of the most successful bands of the late 90's and the early 21st century. In 2021, like Nirvana seven years prior, the Foo Fighters were inducted into the Rock and Roll Hall of Fame. Aside from his continued commitment to music and his general good nature, which has led to his nickname "The Nicest Guy In Rock,"

Grohl is married with three children and has settled in Los Angeles, California.

In 1994, shortly following Cobain's death, Novoselic spoke at a Hoquiam City Council meeting regarding a proposed plan to bring the Lollapalooza music festival to Grays Harbor on August 31. His presence was unannounced, and in addition to advocating for the festival, Novoselic tried to dispel the perception that Cobain hated Aberdeen. "He was a good friend of mine and we used to stay up late at night reminiscing about Aberdeen and Hoquiam," he said. "We've been all around the world and there's a little bit of Aberdeen everywhere."

Now, back in Cobain's hometown, some in the community remember their former resident with adulation. Located just over the Chehalis River, between mileposts one and two on the west side of Highway 12, drivers entering Aberdeen can gaze upon the "Come As You Are" sign, which was installed in 2005 and immortalizes the lyrics of the Nirvana song of the same name. Additionally, in 2015, Aberdeen adopted the Kurt Cobain Memorial Park which is situated near Cobain's childhood home and bordering the Wishkah River.

Years after the death of Kurt Cobain, his music and impact remain a source of passion for generations, subsequent to "X," who continue to experience the power and innocence of a time gone forever.

End Notes

All quotations, unless noted in the text, are attributed below.

Prologue

"Aberdeen feels lethargic..." Everett True, *Nirvana: The Biography*, 2006. (Page 9)

1.

"Up until I was about eight-years-old I had an extremely..." *About a Son*, 2006. (05:56)

"I started to mature..." *Kurt Cobain: Montage of Heck*, 2015. (12:28)

"I was ashamed of my parents..." Jon Savage, "The Lost Interview with Kurt Cobain." *Guitar World*, October 1993.

"I think the sad part of the whole thing is..." *Kurt Cobain: Montage of Heck*, 2015. (15:29 / 17:16)

"something I will do the rest of my life!" Kurt Cobain, *Journals*, 2003. (Page 25)

"I felt more and more alienated..." Michael Azerrad, "Inside the Heart and Mind of Nirvana." *Rolling Stone*, April 16, 1992.

"My mother was a fantastic..." Steffen Chirazi, "LoungeAct." *Kerrang!*, November 29, 1993.

"She also during those first precious..." Kurt Cobain, *Journals*, 2003. (Page 150)

"As soon as I got my guitar..." Michael Azerrad, *Come As You Are*, 1993. (Page 23)

"less manically depressed." Kurt Cobain, *Journals*, 2003. (Page 27)

"They played faster than I ever imagined...". Kurt Cobain, *Journals*, 2003. (Page 57)

"I was always trying to find punk rock..." Jon Savage, "The Lost Interview with Kurt Cobain." *Guitar World*, October 1993.

2.

"He (Cobain) arrived with a huge notebook..." Charles R. Cross, *Heavier Than Heaven: A Biography of Kurt Cobain*, 2001. (Page 72)

"It was a culture shock..." Gillian G. Gaar, *The Rough Guide to Nirvana*, 2009. (Page 8-9)

"totally abrasive" Gina Arnold, "Better Dead Than Cool." *Option*, January / February 1992.

"He was the lead songwriter..." Gillian G. Gaar, *Entertain Us: The Rise of Nirvana*, 2012. (Page 51)

"He was totally into getting wasted..." Everett True, *Nirvana: The Biography*, 2006. (Page 44)

"I was a rodent like, underdeveloped..." Kurt Cobain, *Journals*, 2003. (Page 105)

"shoebox." Michael Azerrad, *Come As You Are: The Story of Nirvana*, 1993. (Page 62)

"I am a totally pampered spoiled bum." Kurt Cobain, *Journals*, 2003. (Page 3)

"Freaking out the red necks." Gina Arnold, "Better Dead Than Cool." *Option*, January / February 1992.

"We had everyone scared of us..." Michael Azerrad, *Come As You Are: The Story of Nirvana*, 1993. (Page 59)

"I wanted a name that was kind of..." Michael Azerrad, *Come As You Are: The Story of Nirvana*, 1993. (Page 62)

3.

"funky space...". Michael Azerrad, *The Amplified Come As You Are: The Story of Nirvana*, 2023. (Page 121)

"a terrible studio..." Gillian G. Gaar, *World Domination: The Sub Pop Records Story*, 2018. (Page 26)

"For about a year..." Everett True, *Nirvana: The Biography*, 2006. (Page 93)

"We just got a phone call..." *Hype!*, 1996. (36:47)

"the paint peeled off the particle board walls..." Michael Azerrad, *Come As You Are: The Story of Nirvana*, 1993. (Page 68)

"(It) went by so fast..." Carrie Borzillo, *Kurt Cobain: The Nirvana Years*, 2013. (Page 20-21)

"He told me, 'There's this kid who came in...'" Carrie Borzillo, *Kurt Cobain: The Nirvana Years*, 2013. (Page 20)

"He seemed delighted..." "Interview with Chad Channing's Parents." *Nirvanaclub*, Unknown Date.

"The first time I sat behind a kit..." Gillian G. Gaar, *Entertain Us: The Rise of Nirvana*, 2012. (Page 107)

"It was really bad..." Charles R. Cross, *Heavier Than Heaven: A Biography of Kurt Cobain*, 2001. (Page 109)

"They never actually said..." Michael Azerrad, *Come As You Are: The Story of Nirvana*, 1993. (Page 79)

4.

"I hung out at the KAOS library..." Everett True, *Nirvana: The Biography*, 2006. (Page 49)

"Focus on the Northwest..." Gillian G. Gaar, *World Domination: The Sub Pop Records Story*, 2018. (Page 32)

"We were making far more commitments..." Greg Prato, *Grunge Is Dead: The Oral History of Seattle Rock Music*, 2009. (Page 132)

"Do you think you could please send us..." Kurt Cobain, *Journals*, 2003. (Page 8)

"Nirvana are beauty incarnate." Everett True, "Love Buzz." *Melody Maker*, February 18, 1989.

"Why don't you trade those guitars for shovels." John D. Luerssen, *Nirvana FAQ: All That's Left to Know About the Most Important Band of the 1990s*, 2014. (Page 94)

"Black Sabbath playing the Knack..." Kurt Cobain, *Journals*, 2003. (Page 33)

"a beautifully soft and mellow, crooning, sleep jingle." Charles R. Cross, *Heavier Than Heaven*, 2001. (Page 118)

"a big smile on his face." Charles R. Cross, *Heavier Than Heaven*, 2001. (Page 118)

5.

"We had nothing else to do." Everett True, *Nirvana: The Biography*, 2006. (Page 113)

"a dry, crunchy, 70s-rock sound." Rob Nash, "No Less Dangerous," *The Independent*, November 19, 2004.

"They were very much about the music at the time..." *Classic Albums: Nirvana - Nevermind*, 2005. (05:35)

"Let's just scream negative lyrics..." Darcey Steinke, "Smashing Their Heads on the Punk Rock," *Spin*, October 1993.

"I picked out good lines..." Darcey Steinke, "Smashing Their Heads on the Punk Rock," *Spin*, October 1993.

"My lyrics are a big pile of contradictions..." Kurt Cobain, *Journals*, 2003. (Page 44)

"And so he was also very careful..." *Kurt Cobain: Montage of Heck*, 2015. (50:06)

"totally intense." Tony Schoengart, "Lamefest '89," *Backlash*, July 1989.

"That show ignited the city's youth..." Mark Yarm, *Everybody Loves Our Town: An Oral History of Grunge*, 2012. (Page 200)

6.

"It's because it was fresh to all of us." Carrie Borozillo, *Kurt Cobain: The Nirvana Years*, 2013. (Page 31)

"They looked so odd..." *Classic Albums: Nirvana - Nevermind*, 2005. (04:14)

"the worst stomach flu you can imagine." Michael Azerrad, *Come As You Are: The Story of Nirvana*, 1993. (Page 66)

"It didn't matter if we played great..." *Classic Albums: Nirvana - Nevermind*, 2005. (27:40)

"We were totally poor..." Michael Azerrad, *Come As You Are: The Story of Nirvana*, 1993. (Page 115)

"He was like a peacock on amphetamines..." Everett True, *Nirvana: The Biography*, 2006. (Page 138)

"mental damages." Michael Azerrad, *Come As You Are: The Story of Nirvana*, 1993. (Page 121)

"I came to the realization..." Mark Yarm, *Everybody Loves Our Town: An Oral History of Grunge*, 2012. (Page 202)

"To be honest..." Clay Tarver, "The Rock 'n' Roll Casualty Who Became a Hero," *New York Times*, July 2, 2013.

"something with real soul." "Kurt Cobain's Blues Influence - Lead Belly." *Cincy Blues Society*, Date Unknown.

"I'd hope that my songs approximate that honesty..." Everett True, *Nirvana: The Biography*, 2006. (Page 146)

"I saw my job as connecting Kurt's voice to the audience." Danny Goldberg, *Serving the Servant: Remembering Kurt Cobain*, 2019. (Page 49)

"When he drinks, he drinks to the point of oblivion..." Michael Azerrad, *Come As You Are: The Story of Nirvana*, 1993. (Page 113)

"People seemed to know who we were..." Gillian G. Gaar, *Entertain Us: The Rise of Nirvana*, 2012. (Page 202)

"a nervous breakdown on stage." Michael Azerrad, *Come As You Are: The Story of Nirvana*, 1993. (Page 127)

"Although generally quiet, he would come alive..." Bruce Pavitt, *Experiencing Nirvana: Grunge In Europe, 1989*, 2013. (Page 55)

"Nirvana was the epiphany of the evening." Bruce Pavitt, *Experiencing Nirvana: Grunge In Europe, 1989*, 2013. (Page 130)

"Nirvana are Sub Pop's answer..." Edwin Pouncey, "The Astoria London," *New Musical Express*, December 16, 1989.

7.

"He had these extreme bipolar mood swings." Gillian G. Gaar, *Entertain Us: The Rise of Nirvana*, 2012. (Page 248)

"he always snaps out of it." Paul Brannigan, *This Is a Call: The Life and Times of Dave Grohl*, 2011. (Page 141)

"Chad would be playing something..." Kurt Stream. "When Nirvana Came To Town." *Madison*, July 2021.

"I got so pissed off at Chad..." Michael Azerrad, *Come As You Are: The Story of Nirvana*, 1993. (Page 140)

"I felt like I'd just killed somebody." Michael Azerrad, *Come As You Are: The Story of Nirvana*, 1993. (Page 139)

"That's one of the things that made Nirvana so great..." Everett True, *Nirvana: The Biography*, 2006. (Page 175)

"I think he pretty much didn't love me..." *Kurt Cobain: Montage of Heck*, 2015. (53:23)

"He was a really good artist..." Greg Prato, *Grunge Is Dead: The Oral History of Seattle Rock Music*, 2009 (Pages 393 / 396)

"looked like dirty fucking biker children." Louis Pattison., "About a Grohl." *New Musical Express*, 2013.

"No thanks. It'll make my teeth bleed." Paul Brannigan, *This Is a Call: The Life and Times of Dave Grohl*, 2011. (Page 145)

"You can't pass up an opportunity..." Michael Azerrad, *Come As You Are: The Story of Nirvana*, 1993. (Page 155)

"were like, 'No, no, no, you're going to be the guy..'" Everett True, *Nirvana: The Biography*, 2006. (Page 197)

"I felt I had something to prove..." Craig McLean, "Dave Grohl: Grohl with It." *Independent*, June 11, 2005.

"Nirvana was now a beast that walked the Earth." Krist Novoselic, *Of Grunge and Government: Let's Fix This Broken Democracy*, 2004. (Page 19)

"That's was the soundtrack to my first six months in Olympia." "Three Feet From God: An Oral History of MTV 'Unplugged.'" *The Ringer*, November 14, 2018.

8.

"We got disconnected..." Charles R. Cross, "Requiem For a Dream," *Guitar World*, October 2001.

"I decided to use heroine..." Kurt Cobain, *Journals*, 2003. (Page 197-198)

"naive but ambitious." Michael Azerrad, *Come As You Are: The Story of Nirvana*, 1993. (Page 161)

"We were very disciplined..." *Classic Albums: Nirvana - Nevermind*, 2005. (05:06)

"I was trying to write the ultimate pop song..." David Fricke, "Kurt Cobain: The Rolling Stone Interview." *Rolling Stone*, January 27, 1994.

"The audience went nuts." Paul Brannigan, *This Is a Call: The Life and Times of Dave Grohl*, 2011. (Page 161)

"We called it 'The Cokewoods'..." Paul Brannigan, *This Is a Call: The Life and Times of Dave Grohl*, 2011. (Page 163)

"We'd work from like noon and then we'd go to Venice Beach..." Author Unknown, "Krist Novoselic: 'You Can't Blame Kurt,'" *New Musical Express*, September 30, 2006.

"He's the best drummer I know..." Paul Brannigan, *This Is a Call: The Life and Times of Dave Grohl*, 2011. (Page 164)

"His performance stunned me..." Butch Vig, "Butch Vig: My Favorite Moments In the Studio." *Rolling Stone*, October 17, 1996.

"Looking back on the production of *Nevermind*..." Michael Azerrad, *Come As You Are: The Story of Nirvana*, 1993. (Page 180)

"hermit in a cave" who would "play his guitar..." *The Amplified Come As You Are: The Story of Nirvana*, 2023. (Page 66)

9.

"With *Nevermind*, Nirvana has certainly succeeded..." Karen Schoemer, "A Band That Deals In Apathy," *The New York Times*, September 27, 1991.

"A dynamic mix of sizzling power chords..." Ira Robbins, "*Nevermind*: Nirvana." *Rolling Stone*, November 28, 1991.

"*Nevermind* is the big American alternative record of the autumn..." Steve Lamacq. "*Nevermind.*" *New Musical Express*, September 21, 1991.

"When Nirvana released *Bleach* all those years ago..." Everett True, "Heaven Up There." *Melody Maker*, September 14, 1991.

"bonded over pharmaceutical." Michael Azerrad, *Come As You Are: The Story of Nirvana*, 1993. (Page 172)

"Kurt Cobain is regarded as a holy man..." Lynn Hirschberg, "Strange Love: The Story of Kurt Cobain and Courtney Love." *Vanity Fair*, September 1, 1992.

"Every time we played, it was blood and guts." E. Barlow, "Dave Grohl: 'I Never Imagined Myself To Be Freddy Mercury'" *The Guardian*, August 16, 2019.

"It just made me feel so stupid..." Michael Azerrad, *Come As You Are: The Story of Nirvana*, 1993. (Page 204)

"He's had but an hour's sleep..." Jerry McCulley, "Spontaneous Combustion" *BAM*, January 10, 1992.

10.

"a litmus test towards our audience." Gillian G. Gaar, *In Utero*, 2006. (Page 3)

"Like a funeral?" "Three Feet From God: An Oral History of MTV 'Unplugged.'" *The Ringer*, November 14, 2018.

"I kept it safe. I kept it like a secret." Chris Heath, "The Nirvana Wars." *Rolling Stone*, June 6, 2002.

"Even in a genre that continues to be degraded by imitators..." David Browne, "You Know You're Right." *Entertainment Weekly*, October 18, 2002.

Bibliography

Books / Periodicals

Anderson, Dawn. "It May Be the Devil and It May Be the Lord....But It Sure As Hell Ain't Human." *Backlash*, August / September 1988.

Anderson, Dawn. "Signing on the Dotted Line and Other Tales of Terror." *Backlash*, March 1991.

Arnold, Gina. "Better Dead Than Cool." *Option*, January / February 1992.

Azerrad, Michael. *The Amplified Come As You Are: The Story of Nirvana*. Harper One, 2023.

Azerrad, Michael. *Come As You Are: The Story of Nirvana*. Doubleday, 1993.

Azerrad, Michael. "Inside the Heart and Mind of Nirvana." *Rolling Stone*, April 16, 1992.

Bernstein, Nils. "Berlin Is Just a State of Mind." *The Rocket*, December 1989.

Borzillo, Carrie. *Kurt Cobain: The Nirvana Years*. Carlton Books, 2013.

Brannigan, Paul. *This Is a Call: The Life and Times of Dave Grohl*. Da Capo Press, 2011.

Browne, David. "You Know You're Right." *Entertainment Weekly*, October 18, 2002.

Chirazi, Steffen. "Lounge Act." *Kerrang!*, November 29, 1993.

Cobain, Kurt. *Journals*. Riverhead Trade, 2003.

Cross, Charles R. *Heavier Than Heaven: A Biography of Kurt Cobain*. Hyperion, 2001.

Cross, Charles R. "Requiem For a Dream." *Guitar World*, October 2001.

Davy, Jeffrey. "The Reading Festival." *Raw!*, October 1991.

Fricke, David. "Kurt Cobain: The Rolling Stone Interview." *Rolling Stone*, January 27, 1994.

Gaar, Gillian G. *Entertain Us: The Rise of Nirvana*. Jawbone Press, 2012.

Gaar, Gillian G. *In Utero*. Continuum, 2006.

Gaar, Gillian G. *The Rough Guide to Nirvana*. Rough Guides, 2009.

Gaar, Gillian G. *World Domination: The Sub Pop Records Story*. BMG, 2018.

Goldberg, Danny. *Serving the Servant: Remembering Kurt Cobain*. Ecco Press, 2019.

Heath, Chris. "The Nirvana Wars." *Rolling Stone*, June 6, 2002.

Hirschberg, Lynn. "Strange Love: The Story of Kurt Cobain and Courtney Love." *Vanity Fair*, September 1, 1992.

Hughes, John C., and Beckwith, Ryan Teague. *On the Harbor: From Black Friday to Nirvana*. The Daily World, 2001.

Jovanovic, Rob. *Nirvana: The Recording Sessions*. Soundcheck Books, 2012.

Kelly, Christina. "Kurt and Courtney Sitting in a Tree." *Sassy*, April 1992.

Lamacq, Steve. "*Nevermind*." *New Musical Express*, September 21, 1991.

Luerssen, John D. *Nirvana FAQ: All That's Left to Know About the Most Important Band of the 1990s*. Backbeat Books, 2014.

McCulley, Jerry. "Spontaneous Combustion." *BAM*, January 10, 1992.

McLean, Craig. "Dave Grohl: Grohl with It." *Independent*, June 11, 2005.

Micalleff, Ken. "Dave Grohl: Returning To His Roots With Probot." *Modern Drummer*, July 2004.

Nash, Rob. "No Less Dangerous," *The Independent*, November 19, 2004.

Novoselic, Krist. *Of Grunge and Government: Let's Fix This Broken Democracy!* RDV Books, 2004.

Pattison, Louis. "About a Grohl." *New Musical Express*, 2013 Special Collector's Edition.

Penn, Nathaniel. *The Moment We Found Nirvana: An Oral History of One of the Greatest Bands of All Time.* GQ Books, 2011.

Perry, Neil. "Live Buzz! SOAS, London." *Melody Maker*, November 4, 1989.

Pouncey, Edwin. "Bleach Review." *New Musical Express*, July 8, 1989.

Pouncey, Edwin. "The Astoria, London." *New Musical Express*, December 16, 1989.

Prato, Greg. *Grunge Is Dead: The Oral History of Seattle Rock Music.* ECW Press, 2009.

Robbins, Ira. "*Nevermind*: Nirvana." *Rolling Stone*, November 28, 1991.

Savage, Jon. "The Lost Interview with Kurt Cobain." *Guitar World*, October 1993.

Schoemer, Karen. "A Band That Deals In Apathy." *The New York Times*, September 27, 1991.

Schoengart, Tony. "Lamefest '89" *Backlash*, July 1989.

St. Thomas, Kurt and Smith, Troy. *Nirvana: The Chosen Rejects.* St. Martin's Press, 2004.

Steinke, Darcey. "Smashing Their Heads on the Punk Rock." *Spin*, October 1993.

Strauss, Neil. "The Downward Spiral: The Last Days of Nirvana's Leader." *Rolling Stone*, June 2, 1994.

Stream, Kurt. "When Nirvana Came To Town." *Madison*, July 2021.

Tarver, Clay. "The Rock 'n' Roll Casualty Who Became a Hero." *The New York Times*, July 2, 2013.

True, Everett. "Heaven Up There." *Melody Maker*, September 14, 1991.

True, Everett. "Latest Wizards from Sub Pop." *Melody Maker*, October 21, 1989.

True, Everett. "Love Buzz." *Melody Maker*, February 18, 1989.

True, Everett. *Nirvana: The Biography*. Omnibus Press, 2006.

True, Everett. "Seattle: Rock City." *Melody Maker*, March 18, 1989.

Vig, Butch. "Butch Vig: My Favorite Moments In the Studio." *Rolling Stone*, October 17, 1996.

Wice, Nathaniel. "How Nirvana Made It." *Spin*, April 1993.

Yarm, Mark. *Everybody Loves Our Town: An Oral History of Grunge*. Crown, 2012.

Unknown Author. "Krist Novoselic: 'You Can't Blame Kurt.'" *New Musical Express*, September 30, 2006.

Movies / Documentaries

About a Son. Schnack, A.J., Balcony Releasing, 2006.

Classic Albums: Nirvana - Nevermind. Smeaton, Bob, Eagle Vision, 2005.

Hype!. Pray, Doug, Cinepix Film Properties, 1996.

Kurt and Courtney. Broomfield, Nick, Capitol Films, 1998.

Kurt Cobain: Montage of Heck. Morgen, Brett, Home Box Office / Universal Pictures, 2015.

Radio / Podcasts

O'Brien, Conan. "Dave Grohl, Krist Novoselic, and *'In Utero'* producer Steve Albini." *Conan O'Brien Needs a Friend.* October 23, 2023.

"Dave Grohl Finds Music's Human Element - In a Machine."*All Things Considered,* hosted by Cornish, Audie and Block, Melissa, NPR, March 8, 2013.

Websites / Website Articles

Barlow, E. (2019, August 16). "Dave Grohl: 'I Never Imagined Myself To Be Freddy Mercury.'" *The Guardian.* https://amp.theguardian.com/music/2019/aug/16/dave-grohl-i-never-imagined-myself-to-be- freddie-mercury

Siegel, A. (2018, November 14). "Three Feet From God: An Oral History of MTV 'Unplugged.'" *The Ringer.* https://

www.theringer.com/platform/amp/music/
2018/11/14/18087878/nirvana-unplugged-oral-history-kurt-
cobain

Unknown Author (Unknown date). "Interview with Chad
Channing's Parents." *Nirvanaclub.* http://
www.nirvanaclub.com/info/nfcinterviews/channing.htm

Unknown Author (Unknown date). "Kurt Cobain's Blues
Influence - Lead Belly." *Cincy Blues Society.* https://
cincyblues.org/education/kurt-cobains-blues-influence-lead-
belly/